I0866506

PASS THE TRAUMA, PLEASE

MY FATHER'S NOT-SO-DEPRESSING HOLOCAUST MEMOIR ABOUT LOVE, LOSS, LAUGHTER, AND LEGACY

TODD DIAMOND

Foreword by Abe Foxman, former director of the ADL

FIG TREE BOOKS

BEDFORD, NEW YORK

Copyright © 2025 Todd Diamond
All rights reserved.

Published in the United States by
Fig Tree Books LLC, Bedford, New York

www.FigTreeBooks.net
An imprint of Mandel Vilar Press, Simsbury, Connecticut

www.MVPublishers.org

Jacket design by Christine Van Bree
Design by Neuwirth & Associates, Inc.

Library of Congress Cataloging-in-Publication
Data Available Upon Request

ISBN number 978-1-941493-33-5
e-ISBN 978-1-941493-36-6

Printed in the United States

1 3 5 7 9 10 8 6 4 2

ABOUT THE AUTHOR'S STATE OF MIND

In 2015, a research team at New York's Mount Sinai Hospital published a paper titled "Holocaust Exposure Induced Intergenerational Effects on FKBP5 Methylation." Their conclusion? "Genetic changes stemming from the trauma suffered by Holocaust survivors are capable of being passed on to their children, the clearest sign yet that one person's life experience can affect subsequent generations."

Huh. Genetically Inherited Holocaust Trauma.

Well, I'll be damned. Doesn't that explain a few things?

For the third generation: Lauren, Reid, and Paxton.
And my father, who survived.

Foreword

ABRAHAM FOXMAN

Former National Director of the Anti-Defamation League (ADL)

SEARCH THROUGH THE ARCHIVES OF HISTORY, AND YOU'LL DISCOVER THAT few events have darkened humanity as deeply as the Holocaust. The atrocities committed are forever inscribed in the collective consciousness. However, as memory fades and remaining survivors depart this life, it becomes more important than ever to continue passing on the narratives and lessons of such heartless evil to this generation and those that will follow.

Today, as in so many times throughout history, we are once again seeing an alarming rise of antisemitism, a resurgence of Holocaust denialism across the globe, and the demonization of Israel, a nation born from the ashes of the Holocaust. If we have learned anything from the past, it's that hateful rhetoric and disinformation can engender violence, inflame intolerance, and lay the groundwork for genocide. If left unchallenged, it will certainly lead to disastrous consequences.

As the former National Director of the Anti-Defamation League, and as a survivor myself, I have not only been a witness to the enduring legacy of antisemitism but I've also made it my life's work to inform the world, through rigorous data gathering and documentation, about the menacing recurrences of extremism. It's a brutal and unsettling endeavor, but it is vital that we catalog acts of bigotry and violence against Jews as well as other ethnicities confronting immoral forces.

In addition to hard, factual evidence, we must never cease to preserve and disseminate our personal stories of survival. Against a backdrop of expanding indifference and a receding interest in traditional Holocaust education, it is imperative to create space for innovative technologies and unconventional voices. What is needed more than ever are new resonant narratives that engage wider, more diverse audiences with different perspectives that illuminate the past in such a way as to help us understand better the effects of these tragedies on succeeding generations—both those of descendants of survivors and those who were not affected personally. Their stories deserve to be heard. They are bridges between what has been and what could be, vibrant reminders of the complex ways trauma manifests and is transmitted across generations.

Pass the Trauma, Please isn't just about the death camps, the gas chambers, the incomprehensible evil. It's about the Holocaust and its aftershocks. The unrelenting ripple effect of a unique trauma that echoes through children raised in the long shadow of tragedy.

Indeed, this story does examine the burden of memory, the inheritance of bruised narratives passed down like heirlooms. But the story doesn't end there. It's about resilience, too, about the brazen human spirit that refuses to let the bonds of family be extinguished. Most importantly, the book is about carving out a life and managing to find light and humor amidst the wreckage. A testament to the power of memory.

Preface

Number one: Going number one saved my father's life.

Number two: Going number two saved my father's life.

Introduction

I'M A SLOW WRITER IN A RACE AGAINST THE INEVITABLE DATE OF MY FATHER'S death. He is one of the last remaining Holocaust survivors. He is ninety three years old as I write this. He is healthy; he is wise. He insisted I tell the world that he still gets it up (with a little boost from Viagra).

Writing his story is tough for me. I can't shake the feeling that nearly every child with a parent connected to this unique history has already published a book about it or created a provocative work of genocide-themed art that hangs in a museum or is proudly displayed in the home of a prominent Jewish family on the Upper East Side of Manhattan.

At this point, I've got a few index cards with general thoughts and outlines. I am way behind, but my father is a survivor, so I expect him to hang around long enough to read some of it, hopefully most of it, and ideally a first draft. My father knows I'm attempting to write his story. He did have one request. He said, "Please, just not another Holocaust memoir with the long-winded descriptions and elaborate accounts of the smells in the Ghetto, the corpses. Everyone knows this already. Elie Wiesel, Primo Levy, Anne Frank, that guy who wrote the comic book about the mouse, they all covered it. Spielberg, too, such a genius, so do something different. Don't be afraid to slip in a few jokes. What do you call it again . . . that bullshit you always say . . . ? Oh yeah, write something poster-punk." He meant to say, post-punk. My father concluded his appeal by saying, "And besides, you're no Elie Wiesel."

Indeed. The truth is, I am an advertising copywriter. This book is different, it's difficult, and I'm afraid I won't meet the deadline.

San Mateo, California

DECEMBER 2020

TRAVELING NORTH ON EL CAMINO REAL. I'M RUNNING THIRTY MINUTES late. It's what I'm known for, and not fondly, mind you. But this time, I had a respectable reason. I had to stop; there was no way to resist the gravitational tug of Christmas TV memories, more specifically, Charlie Brown and his indelible evergreen screw up. It's the classic wintry tale of a blockheaded boy and a fragile fir, neither one possessing a solid foundation—two outsiders out in the cold that are charmingly drawn and drawn to one another.

Certain Schultz sequences cling hard to the heart, never to be dislodged. For example, the hark-the-heralded conclusion of *A Charlie Brown Christmas*, when the children gaze upward toward the heavens, their mouths stretched open as wide as frat bros participating in a hazing ritual involving dangerous amounts of upside-down alcohol consumption. The mean-spirited youth in the show are eventually shown the light, the true meaning of the season.

A few animated cells later, the mood shifts. The taunting mob suddenly embraces the boy and warmly exclaims, "Merry Christmas, Charlie Brown!" Chuck's scraggy tree, now wrapped in the security of Linus's blanket along with an ornament that pulled down a spindly branch, miraculously brings everyone together.

That's what compelled me to turn sharply into the Christmas tree lot. Or what was left of it. Just five trees remained, meek and withered, mostly brown, and Charlie Brown–esque. All the trees had a serious case of pine-needle bedhead. I drove away with a slightly moldering conifer. Of course, I worked a deal; you can't fight genetics.

Two seasons of holiday specials had aired since my last visit to California. What got me there after all that time wasn't just the stewardship of a navigation app. I was returning to celebrate my father's birthday. He is a ninety-three-year-old Holocaust survivor. He survived another year. Allow me to repeat that one more time for all my Nazi and Holocaust-denying readers: He. Survived. Another. Year.

Frankly, I was surprised the digital North Star didn't throw a tantrum and tell me to make up my fucking mind while ranting in a harsh accent like the ones you'd hear in Jersey Shore or Bensonhurst. The software's frustration would be entirely justified because I kept making it reroute and then reroute again. Although I was running behind, as I tend to do, I was determined to voyage down a few memory lanes to seek out the house that sheltered me after my divorce. Quick word about our dotcom-bust-era bust up: This disunion was supposed to be the model for all other divorces, but it didn't quite turn out that way. It could have—it started out in a balanced, mediator-driven direction until we both ignored the suggested scenic routes and engaged teams of legal advisers rivaling O.J. Simpson's squad. In our defense, I've always believed the situation escalated into radioactive territory due to the relentless pressure of certain "friends" who turned into Vichy-like collaborators as well as the accomplished guidance of her sibling, a clever lawyer and a rather disputatious sister.

EXHIBIT A: After spending our weekend together, I dropped the kids off with my ex-spouse. Her sister and children were at my ex-house visiting from Washington, DC. My ex-brother-in-law was there as well; he's cool, I miss him. My ex's sister wasted no time. She immediately gets up in my face and begins her cross examination: "So, I hear you have a girlfriend," she says in a most prosecutorial way. I looked past her before answering, noticing that they were traveling with their very attractive nanny—the kind of household support staff that would sound alarm bells and issue infidelity warnings from neighbors.

"I do," I replied.

Fans of courtroom TV dramas take note: Without any delay, her finger shoots up, comes way too close to my face, and she blurts out, "I do! Two words that *you* should never speak again." *Oooooooh, good burn, counselor.* It made me laugh. The woman is tough, but she's also funny. "Ouch. Nice one," I said, and drifted over to her husband to say goodbye. He was sitting on my ex-sofa watching football on my ex-TV. He'd heard the exchange and kindly conveyed a sympathetic shoulder shrug. How many times per week did he offer this gesture to those who crossed his wife's path?

His trapezius muscles must be huge.

"Oh, hey, before I go, I have another two words, but they're for you ex-brother." There was a brief moment of silence as I made eye contact with the nanny. I gave her an exaggerated wink, looked back at him, and said these two words: "Jude Law."

You see, at that time, Jude was caught up in a tawdry celebrity-cheats-with-the-nanny scandal. I dropped the mic and got out of there.

Honestly, I really wasn't expecting the abrupt divorce detour that would take us down a costly toll road. My ex, after all, has the logic and reasoning that comes with being an architect—she builds lovely things. This time, however, we followed a flawed blueprint. We could have carefully dismantled what remained, but instead, we allowed the demolition experts to take the lead on the project. Well, that's my point of view. Perhaps her side views things a little differently.

Huh, you think?

Look, I realize that on the spectrum of trauma, my post-marriage struggle for economic survival is a few notches below Jewish genocide and a teeny bit less tormenting than my father's confrontations with the Gestapo—still, one man's Gestapo is another man's ex-wife's divorce attorney.

To all my divorced parent readers . . . I mostly survived.

Since I wasn't ready to spring the D-word on the kids, I told Reid, my five-year-old son, and Lauren, my eight-year-old daughter, that the small house I rented after moving out was our family's "guest house" and that I was hanging there temporarily to be closer to my San Francisco office.

Young hippie boy bought the story. Cynical girl? Yeah right. One thing my daughter noted about the humble abode was that it was situated near a bowling alley, which really didn't surprise her at all, because as she put it, "Bowling is the universal divorced-dad thing to do with his kids."

"Your destination is on the right."

Memories from the Guest House on Poplar Street

SAN MATEO, CALIFORNIA

I PARKED ACROSS THE STREET FROM THE TWO-BEDROOM, ONE-BATH house at the end of a cul-de-sac and rolled down the passenger side window. A shaft of late afternoon sunlight intruded, illuminating a once-invisible layer of dust clinging to the rental car dashboard. Other than a new paint color on the front door, everything about the house was pretty much the same.

Just a quick five-minute drive to the bowling alley, the Guest House was the landing pad that caught me after ejecting out of a marriage that caught fire as it was hurtling toward earth.

As I sat there, I remembered how Lauren pimped out her loft bed—the summit of the Ikea bed-on-top-with-space-below-for-a-desk contraption that she shared with her brother. This was the first time they had ever roomed together. It could have been a disaster, but it kind of worked out. Lauren strung lights around the bed frame and hung bohemian drapes from the ceiling to create a luxe, personal environment. Below was Reid's domain, which consisted of a large dog bed left behind by the previous tenant, along with a collection of my son's school drawings haphazardly taped to the wall. Sorry, little man. In the haste of setting up a new life, only one mattress arrived. Thankfully, his human sleep accommodation showed up the following weekend of the every-other-weekend arrangement. Today, Reid is a long-distance hiker and backpacker. Perhaps his time on the canine cushion influenced his bold outdoor pursuits.

I recently learned that Lauren and Reid share a few hearty laughs about my disorganized start to a new life. If I could hack into their text exchanges, I would drop this bit of perspective into the text bubbles, sans emoji. Use your words, children:

REID: Soooooooo funny! OMG, Papa had almost nothing in the "Guest House."

LAUREN: Right!? Soooooooooooooooo funny.

PAPA: Actually, looking back on it, I didn't take anything when I moved out. Left it all behind to minimize the disruption to your lives.

REID: Right!? I think the only thing he took was a cereal bowl and a spoon.

PAPA: OMFG, I just remembered something . . . business was hurting at the time. My ad agency almost went bankrupt due to the slow recovery from the dotcom crash.

LAUREN: Some clothes, I suppose. Everything else he had to buy. Really, EVERYTHING!

PAPA: And yet, for you all to stay as comfortable as possible, I took on a lot of debt.

LAUREN: Yeah, come to think of it, Papa left us all the stuff. And he gave us money, probably way more than he could afford.

PAPA: Way more . . .

THE EX: HEY TODD, NOT ALL YOUR STUFF WAS LEFT BEHIND. YOU MADE SURE TO GRAB YOUR BOX OF DISSOCIATIVE DISORDERS BEFORE MOVING OUT!

Shit. Shit! How did she hack into this hacked revisionist conversation? She's right, of course. Man, she's good.

So anyway . . . here's an idea for Ikea management: *Divorced Dad Aisle*—everything a newly single parent could possibly need in a single beeline of a shopping cart.

DOCTOR'S NOTE

Dear Ex-Spouse,

Please excuse Todd's dissociative behaviors. Our research demonstrated significantly elevated symptoms of Holocaust Survivor Offspring (HSO).

—Sincerely, Dr. Halligan and Dr. Yehuda

Memory Two from the Guest House:

"POPPY DAVE . . . PAPA IS SLEEPING WITH HIS GIRLFRIEND'S MOM."

DIANA'S MOTHER CAME TO VISIT. DURING HER STAY, MY FATHER CALLED to say hi to his grandkids. When Reid got on the phone, he said this: "Hi Poppy Dave. Yeah, I'm having fun. Diana's mom is a really good cook. Last night, Papa slept with Diana, and the night before that, he slept with Diana's mom, and tonight, he is probably sleeping with Diana again, or maybe her mom." I imagine my father just rolled his eyes and figured there was about a 10 percent chance that his grandson was speaking the truth.

Memory Three from the Guest House:

THE HOUSE HAD ONE OUTSTANDING FEATURE: A STEAM SHOWER. I RARELY used it because, well, obviously you know what it reminded me of, right?

"Recalculating route."

The event that kept pulling me back to the original route, back to this place after an extended absence, was dinner in a new neighborhood which suddenly appeared atop a landfill in the marshes of the San Francisco Bay. The restaurant was chosen to celebrate my father's upcoming birthday. Dining out this evening would be me, my older brother, Steve, and my father, David.

Before entering the restaurant, I glanced at my watch.

Cool, I was only twenty minutes late.

Chinese Restaurant

FOSTER CITY, CALIFORNIA

MY FATHER AND BROTHER ARE SEATED AT A TABLE. I WALK UP BEHIND MY father and kiss the top of his head.

I hold him tightly, then go to hug my brother.

STEVE

So, how's that book coming, Todd? You gonna finish it by Dad's birthday?

DAD

Steve . . . you know your brother is always late. So . . . maybe when I'm one hundred? Pfff, next month I only turn ninety. Apparently not such a big deal. Oh, I just remembered . . . after dinner, I need to stop at Walgreens to pick up my new, much-much stronger blood pressure medication. Anyway, Todd, you just take your sweet time writing my survivor story.

I pull out a thick notebook.

TODD

Ah, funny, Pops. I'm trying. I think it's almost done, but there are still a few things about your story that I'm not exactly clear on. You good talking about it tonight?

DAD

Oh, I see. Some Holocaust chit-chat over sweet and sour pork? That feeling a little un-kosher to either of you? Sure, sure, go ahead, but let's order first. I'm starving because surprise . . . you were late. And listen, you better be accurate. Don't screw up the facts you're writing about me. And another thing—don't glorify my story, don't exaggerate, and don't turn me into a general if I'm a sergeant, know what I mean?

TODD

I know exactly what you mean, and I promise to be in full compliance. So . . . permission to interrogate?

DAD

As if I have a choice?

Steve picks up his menu, flips through the pages.

STEVE

Should we start with the usual white-people dishes?

TODD

Order whatever you want, Steve, and don't forget the sweet and sour 'in-memoriam' for Mom.

My father puts his cup of tea to the side.

DAD

Hard to believe she's been gone five years now. I should've been dead, too, you know, long ago. But somehow, here I am. I don't know. Maybe it's fate, or luck, or outsmarting the Nazis.

My father clasps his hands and looks upward.

DAD

Or maybe it's . . . a leak on the roof.

TODD

Huh? Are you making a reference to *Fiddler on the Roof*?

DAD

Wha . . . ? No. Look, the ceiling tile, it's got a big water stain. But since you bring it up . . . as Tevye said, 'Traditions, traditions.' Without our traditions, our lives would be as shaky as a . . . come on boys, sing it with me—

TODD AND STEVE

(half-heartedly) Fiddler on the roof.

DAD

Eh, a little off key, but not bad for three hangry Jews. And speaking of traditions, on this Sunday night, like so many other Sunday nights before it, these last remaining members of a small Jewish family, made smaller by hate-filled madmen, will sit in a Chinese restaurant and eat and eat until we must loosen our pants.

Warsaw Ghetto, Poland

EARLY 1940s

MY FATHER TIGHTENED HIS PANTS.

He cinched a belt made of rope until the waistband with the secret interior pocket finally made contact with a waistline that was in fast retreat. If his exhausted body could summon enough breath to sing for passengers while riding trolley cars on the Christian side of the Ghetto wall, he'd earn enough money to finance the purchase of pharmaceuticals. These life saving (or what-was-left-of-life) medications would be tucked inside the hidden pocket of his trousers and then turned over to his father—a doctor—so he could continue treating patients on the other side of the wall.

For my father, a child smuggler in the Warsaw Ghetto, starvation had an upside; a diminishing body meant you could crawl your way to the outside through smaller, less-detectable tunnels and return like an elongated shadow at dusk.

There were so many hungry eyes constantly on watch, ready to rat out anyone seen slipping under the ten-foot-high ghetto walls. An extra loaf of bread, a warm coat, or perhaps the shoes taken from an apprehended smuggler would be the informant's wretched reward. If you were a Jew, if you were caught, you no longer needed those comforts. Typically, a dehumanizing example would be made for other ghetto residents to see; most likely, you were shot dead in the street, publicly hanged, or worse: put on a train.

Unless you were my father, a twelve-year-old smuggler whose father had saved a Polish police captain from a very serious illness. The doctor turned to his grateful patient, seeking a way to help protect his son. The boy desperately needed false identity papers in case of an arrest. The police captain came through; the Jewish boy was given a new identity and a Christian name that ended with the letter i.

A last name ending in y would have killed the boy.

Y is the only circumcised letter in the Polish alphabet. The boy, my father, David Diamentstein, was now Taduesz Lipski. Eventually, the kid with the newski nameski would be captured by the Gestapo, but because he had fake identity papers in his non-hidden pocket, he survived.

He survived.

Warsaw, Poland

EARLY 1940s

MY FATHER JUMPED OFF AT THE LAST TROLLEY CAR STOP BEFORE IT ENTERED the Ghetto—just like any other "Christian" boy would do. There was great risk in the routine: you disembark, walk about a quarter mile, pray you don't get caught, then reinsert yourself back into the horrors on the other side of the wall. If you get there, you say a prayer of thanks that you made it and then, you complete the routine with one last prayer: that you'll make it out again.

It had been a long day of Trolley Car Karaoke. His set list included Polish folk songs about flowers, wedding celebrations, and the pleasures of regional birds and farming. It was a successful day, too, because enough nationalistic noise poured out of him to earn the zloty required to purchase medications for his father's patients. The pharmacist and my grandfather had a long-standing relationship. But now, whenever my father entered the store, no questions were asked (you never knew who'd be listening). No small talk. No, "How's your father?" It was completely transactional, as if each of them had taken just the right dosage of pharmaceutical grade memory eraser to expunge all familiarity and all traces of pleasant memories from past visits. My father simply handed over the money and the list, and the pharmacist handed over the drugs.

Not all of his hard-sung earnings went toward medicines. Some of it was used to procure apples and potatoes, supplemental purchases that would go to his mother and father who anxiously waited for him in their compressed Ghetto apartment. Some of the haul was eaten on the job, usually a sandwich.

Ugh, those tween smugglers. So selfish.

Chinese Restaurant

FOSTER CITY, CALIFORNIA

Steve is pushing rice onto his plate, a fluffy platform to soak up our over-sauced, white-folk fare.

STEVE

Hey, Todd, do you ever recall Dad singing Polish songs when we were growing up?

TODD

No way. All I ever heard was his pervy crooning, which should've been slapped with an E for explicit lyrics. Dad, you remember some of your greatest dirty hits from the sixties and seventies, don't you?

DAD

Sha, sha, what are you talking about?

Steve breaks into a K-Tel Records announcer voice:

STEVE

This incredible collection includes chart toppers like, 'She Loves to Grab My Schvantz' and the smash hit, 'Oy, the Shiksa Has a Hairy Vagina.'

My father attempts to wave away this verbal ribbing. I seamlessly pick up imitating the K-Tel Records announcer:

TODD

That's right, Steve, and many more unforgettable tunes including, 'Groys Schmeckel Mit a Blister.' And who can forget the delightful ballad, 'I'm a Pimp, My Wife is a Kurva.'

TODD

(turns to his father)
Dad, that's Yiddish for prostitute, right?

DAD

Yes, putzface.

TODD

(continues the K-tel schtick)
Or the rollicking parody, 'Titty Titty Bang Bang,' a song I suspect young Weird Al Yankovic heard you sing in the shower.

DAD

Couple of comedians, my sons. Hey, where's the waiter? Maybe I will have that scotch now.

Electchester Apartments, Queens

LATE 1970s

IF YOU HAD HEARD THE SONGS, I GUESS YOU MIGHT CALL HIM A DIRTY OLD man. But I have to cut my old man some slack. The culture was looser back when I was a kid. It was a swinging, chauvinistic time, which helps explain the nasty tunes sung mainly in English with flashes of Yiddish.

You might be wondering if his gift of song was passed down from one generation to the next. Yes, it was. It pours out of me in showers and also while I'm shaving. Would I care to share any of my original compositions? Not a chance. Stumbling around the internet over the years has warped me; therefore, sharing any of my obscene tunes would plunge this book to that rarely perused shelf where tales of literary erotica press hard against one another.

Some things are better left unwritten.

In addition to the ditties about the titties, I also tracked a complementary behavior of my father: incessantly grabbing my mom's boobs. Yes, they were large. In fact, she had custom-made bras to reduce their appearance. If you pulled out a random 8mm film from the shoebox containing our family's home movies—even the one titled *Disneyland Trip*—you'd be guaranteed to see at least two instances of boob-grab. In the Disney example, the gropes occurred at the one-minute and three-minute marks: first, in front of Snow White's Scary Adventure, and then, outside of It's a Small World, a location that I believe was intentionally selected for the irony. The way I saw it, each squeeze conveyed my father's deep affection for his wife.

So yeah, my father's *Greatest Dirty Hits of the 60s and 70s* were indeed offensive and certainly not intended for all audiences. But they were also hilarious and joyful compositions, simple and unabashed, completely free from the rattling sounds of trolley cars and the ear-splitting dissonance of survival.

Holocaust Unplugged.

I first learned about my father's Holocaust history on Father's Day, toward the closing years of the 1970s. We were sitting in the living room. One of his favorite Herb Alpert records was playing on the stereo—the one with the seductive woman on the album cover who is covered in whipped cream. The song came to an end—I think it was "Love Potion No. 9." As the turntable needle hung in the groove between songs, I finally found the courage to ask him about his past, a subject he rarely discussed.

You get it, right? Using Father's Day as the big dramatic cliché moment when you turn to your Euro-dad and ask him who he is and what his origin story is? The movie *Yentl* was a few years from its release date, but the crescendo-loaded, tear-jerking smasher, "Papa Can You Hear Me" (Streisand, not the *Glee* cast version) would have swelled in the background, overtaking Herb Alpert and his brass as I put forth the grand question: "Dad, who are you?"

I knew our family had some connection to the Holocaust and to the Israeli War of Independence, but my father never shared any of it. And honestly, I was never curious enough to ask. But after the subject came up in a school lecture, I saw how deeply it affected some of the students, especially the young women. They were sobbing. And then it occurred to me that I could exploit my personal history in two ways:

A. Lure women with a tragic family history angle.

B. Get out of jams.

In fact, as I have taught my own children: if you're ever in a pickle, like being late on a homework assignment or if you flunk a test, then it is time to "Release the Holocaust Story from its cage." Tell the teacher that you had to help your tyrannized grandfather, a Holocaust survivor, to blah, blah, and blah. Works every single time.

To fully leverage our family's story, I had to understand it and really load up on the details. Yes, I was a teenage Holocaust opportunist, but I was also genuinely interested in finally knowing more about my father, which consequently, might reveal things about myself.

So . . .

"Dad, who are you . . . ?"

It was followed by a barrage of other questions. Some were basic timeline queries; others got into the touchy-feely emotional zone, a place where my father clearly did not want to roam. He sat there in silence, absorbing my line of questioning.

"Wait here," he said firmly. "Actually, go to your bedroom. I'll meet you there."

My father got up from the sofa. He walked across the lime-green shag carpet to his bedroom with the sky-blue shag carpet. I waited in my bedroom, standing barefoot on gold shag carpet spun from chemically infused fibers permanently stained with chemically processed foods. This was the late seventies after all, and weird science had taken up residence in our family's food supply and within the fabrics of our lives.

With strands of gold between my toes, I waited for my father. I was freaking out a bit, wondering what the hell he was about to reveal. To help ratchet down the anxiety, I stared out the window, hoping to catch a glimpse of my neighbor doing torso twists and squats in her bra and girdle; it was always a fantastic soft-core show for this peeping Todd. However, my timing was off. The constricting garment routine was not happening. So, I turned to face the Wall of Greatness: a wood panel terrain that, over the years, had been covered with painstakingly vetted pictures of people and places that meant everything to me. It began with

Sports Illustrated and *LIFE* magazine, each image carefully removed from the glossy pages with surgical precision.

Other photos that made it to the wall came from the original internet: our family's World Book Encyclopedia collection. This resulted in several volumes looking as if they had been attacked by geometry-loving booklice with a unique ability to carve out impeccable rectangles and squares. In a way, the Wall of Greatness was like an archaeological site, each layer cataloging cultural history. As you dig further down through the decades, one can determine the things that were meaningful to a typical kid from Flushing, New York.

A few years later, photos from the rock magazines *CREEM* and *CIRCUS* took the wood-panel stage, fraternizing with gaudy, polychromatic blacklight posters—trippy works of head shop art which paired perfectly with an in-the-dark listening to *Dark Side of the Moon*. Included in this collection was a giant eyeball, a skeleton riding a Harley chopper, and Popeye doing it doggie-style with Olive Oyl—a serious lapse of aesthetic judgment. Sorry, but I yam what I yam. Also, thanks Mom and Dad for never censoring any of the exhibits that graced the Wall of Greatness.

Back to the surface. Following their extrication, each picture went through a meticulous method of Scotch Tape hanging: a carefully measured adhesive piece in each corner, plus a small strip at the center top and another small strip at the center bottom.

All corners. Center top. Center bottom. Six pieces in all.

Looking back on how the pictures were displayed, the earliest layer of the wall reminded one of Gertrude Stein's salon. That is, if she lived in apartment 6J on 162nd Street instead of 27 rue de Fleurus. Rather than gazing at Matisse and Picasso, you'd stand back and admire key members of what would become The Miracle Mets—those pinstriped torches who ignited hope for a kid who could see Shea Stadium from his building rooftop, one of the many viscid tar beaches that overlooked our housing project.

Shea was no Yankee Stadium, but so what? The less-legendary stadium hosted the Beatles. You hear that, Yankee Stadium? The

B-E-A-T-L-E-S. Hysterical girls, revolutionary rockers, and the New York Mets, all under the same bright stadium lights.

And now (echo: *now . . . now . . . now . . .*), the starting line up (echo: *up . . . up . . . up . . .*) for the 1968-1969 Wall of Greatness (*cheering crowd, rallying organ music*).

First up, Jerry Koosman and Tom Seaver on the mound, fluid arms frozen in mid-pitch by fast shutter speed. Next, we salute Tug McGraw hurling late-inning missiles, providing relief for the mighty arms of Koosman and Seaver. Now, let's give it up for Ed Kranepool, Al Weis, and Buddy Harrelson: the steel-faced guardians of the infield.

And of course, Cleon Jones, Tommie Agee, and Art Shamsky: the impenetrable outfield. Oh, if the name Shamsky sounds Jewish, it is. A Jewish professional athlete is a rare thing indeed. Doesn't come around too often, kind of like a comet, a Hebrew comet: Chhhhhalley's Comet.

In those years, athletes weren't the only heroic figures occupying space on the Wall of Greatness. There are two other people worth mentioning: Robert Kennedy and Martin Luther King Jr. My intense feelings for these men landed their images slightly above the rest—regal and overseeing all. But that did not mean they escaped the rigorous taping process:

All corners. Center top. Center bottom. Six pieces in all.

During that period, the Wall of Greatness took a fatal hit. Martin Luther King Jr. was shot while standing on a motel balcony. Shortly after that, another fatal blow; while walking through a hotel kitchen, Robert Kennedy was struck by three bullets. Both men taken down by what they'd stood up to.

At the time of each shooting and for many months after, I would check and recheck those MLK and RFK photos to be sure they hadn't been knocked off the wall by assassins. But no matter how much I told myself not to worry, I just couldn't shake the fear that they might drop. Reinforcement was required. I went into my father's toolbox and grabbed a roll of heavy-duty electrical tape. It was strong enough to withstand high heat, so hopefully it could endure the conflicts and confusion of the time. I placed a second layer on top of the original taping. Six black pieces that looked like six tiny black armbands.

All corners. Center top. Center bottom. A sticky memorial. And reassurance that those two great men would never fall away from me.

You'd think a wall with the word "Greatness" in its name would have some girth. It didn't. In fact, it was a very thin wall, one that surprisingly did not collapse under the weight of the wood paneling. This flimsy barrier was the only thing separating my bedroom from my parents' bedroom, which meant I could clearly hear my father rummaging around in his closet, searching for the artifacts from his past.

I also used to hear a headboard slamming against that thin wall every Saturday night (no nookie on school nights). There was this one time when I heard my mother exclaim during their lovemaking, "Dave, Dave, I feel like I'm floating," and then, right in the middle of her frisky-time acclamation, I heard a loud THUD. Apparently, my parents were too cheap to shell out the money for a proper king-sized mattress and box spring set—something about the sheets costing too much. So, they put two twins next to one another, but the beds and the box springs didn't always stay together; they'd split apart, creating a gravitational vortex that would suck my parents to the ground. See what I'm saying? Actually, please don't see what I just said.

Returning to the sounds from the closet on the other side of the wall . . . my father was speaking and grunting in his typical mix of Yiddish and English, but it was not lyrical at all. I heard a lot of sighing, and then he kept repeating, "You motherfuckers. You Nazi motherfuckers," while making his way to my bedroom. After a brief trek across green and blue shag carpets, my father paused, took a deep breath, and slowly pushed open the door to my room.

He was holding a worn brown envelope. He pulled out a distressed document. It looked historic, like an old passport or a bank savings account book.

"Open it, but be careful. It's fragile," he cautioned. On the book's cover was a swastika. Inside was a picture of my father, a twelve-year-old kid who looked more like a twenty-year-old man. The name attached to the photo wasn't David Diamentstein, which was my father's Polish birth name.

Instead, it said Tadeusz Lipski.

"Lipski? What is that? Who is Tadeusz Lipski? Is that you, Dad? Is this your fake ID?"

Manhattan, 54th Street and 8th Avenue

LATE 1970s

WE BOTH HAD FAKE IDS.

My false identity took me into a series of hellish zones with velvet ropes and tyrannical selection processes—pulsing places infested with a few A-list celebrities, several B-list celebrities, and hysterical throngs pleading to be let in.

Conversely, my father's fake papers kept him out of places where the ultimate fate of panic-stricken people was promptly determined by a hand inside of a black leather glove, a hand that pointed to the right or to the left, a hand that should have been trembling but was not.

Chinese Restaurant

FOSTER CITY, CALIFORNIA

My father whips up his usual egg roll condiment blend: 75 percent hot mustard, 25 percent duck sauce, and a splash of scotch.

TODD

Why'd you keep it a secret, Dad? I mean twenty years . . .

STEVE

Yeah, Dad, if you'd blurted out your story sooner, maybe Todd would have a couple more chapters by now.

My father glares at me, slowly takes a bite of his egg roll. Puts it down. Then picks it back up and uses it as a pointer. Duck sauce flies onto me.

DAD

Putz, I have several survivor friends, right? And their kids? Fucked up. Deeeeep therapy. Why? Because all they ever heard from the moment they could sit up in their crib was Holocaust this and Holocaust that. It was nonstop.

I understand, I do, but I could see the damage being done. So, I chose not to traumatize my own kids with the memories. No, that was something I would carry and dump onto you guys when I decided it was the right time.
Achh, I'm telling you, those poor kids.

I wipe the duck sauce from my shirt with my middle finger, defiantly lick it off.

TODD

Dad, I could've handled it, whatever you told me. It would not have fucked me up.

DAD

Oh really? I struggled whether to tell you when you first asked. What a mess you were with the makeup and the eyeliner, the pierced ears, dancing half-naked at discos, coming home as I was leaving for work. You think I didn't know about all the coke going up your nose? I'm trained by the Haganah, *tatala*, I see everything. Oh, you were fucked up, and that's without my Holocaust nightmares crammed into your head.

Steve uses chopstick to mimic eyeliner application.

STEVE

Lancôme, right?

Manhattan, 54th and 8th

LATE 1970s

AT THIS PARTICULAR TIME, OUR FATHER-AND-SON RELATIONSHIP HAD BEEN collapsing as quickly as my septum. Poor guy—how strange it must have been for him to see me returning home from nights out in Manhattan just as he was leaving for work. The eyeliner streaks running down my cheeks (which always looked like Rorschach tests to me) didn't help to ease the situation.

We had several of these awkward early morning encounters. I'd come back from a club, and my father, blisteringly disgusted, would push past me on the stoop in front of our building and not utter a word. Well, maybe I did hear him say something under his breath—a slur associated with the men who had pink triangles sewn onto their striped prison uniforms during Nazi occupations.

Fact is, I was going through a rough time. Life had quickly descended into the black-and-white (and white powder) decadence of Hasse Perrson and Allan Tannenbaum photos.

All because Ilene dumped me.

It was summer, just a few months after we un-virginized in her bedroom as her hot mom was taking a warm bath down the hall, and just a few weeks before the start of our freshman year at Queens College. As her dumping ground, Ilene "I Scream" (that girl was loud when we were doing it) chose the sidewalk outside of the Music Box, a used record store that set me on the righteous path of rock-and-roll vinyl.

A major slice of my teen-life pie chart was spent at the Music Box, getting schooled by the Frampton-haired curator, an expert on Bowie and Reed, Mott the Hoople, T-Rex, Elton, King Crimson, Pink Floyd, Led Zeppelin, Zappa, Hendrix, Nektar, and The Stones. He directed us to the B-sides, to the bootlegs, to the solo efforts; he presented us with rare live recordings from Japan. He even selected the album that I would play as I slid in and out of Ilene "I Scream" for the very first time. It was Bowie's *Low* album, recorded in Berlin, and let me tell you, I tore down Ilene's wall. Not to brag, but I held back the blast all the way to "Sound and Vision"—almost a full seven minutes—nearly half of side one before virgin-no-more.

How could she kick *me*, a promising city college kid to the litter-filled curb? I was a pretty good boyfriend. Sure, there was the period of time when, almost daily, my friends and I would show up at Ilene's apartment, and they'd wait in the car and get high. I'd go up to see her and do her, tenderly kiss her goodbye, and then leave to go hang out with my patient stoner friends. At least I kissed Ilene goodbye.

Unlike other guys who were in a similarly structured relationship, my friends never got the sordid details, never had the scent of Ilene's private parts still clinging to my fingers and waved beneath their nostrils. You see what I'm saying here? Good boyfriend material.

Good got even better. We evolved into a proper couple, going on proper dates, making out in my Ford Pinto in scenic spots that were far away from chain-link fencing.

We'd feed each other pizza slices from Gloria's after sneaking into the movies on Roosevelt Avenue. No wham or bam or thank you, ma'am. It was more romantic. What's not to love? Wasn't that enough?

It wasn't enough. I was too late to maturity. Ilene wanted more, and because I never understood exactly what "more" was, the girl whose picture hangs in my Hall of Firsts, plunged a breakup dagger deep into my still-developing heart.

I bled all over the place. I was desperate. Shit, I think I might have loved her. How could I not? Ilene was a Bowie fanatic who would get incredibly turned on by his album cover art. There were a few in particular that really cranked up the heat inside her gripping designer jeans: *Pin Ups, Aladdin Sane,* and *Diamond Dogs*. If you ever saw those twelve inches of rockrotica, you understand exactly what I mean.

Music. I needed the music, because only music would get me through this bleak stretch of loneliness wrapped in a dispiriting darkness. So, I went to the Music Box for a vinyl prescription. The curator took out his pad and wrote me a scrip for "Don't Think Twice, It's All Right." Mr. Dylan's miracle breakup elixir to the rescue. Take fifty listens and call Dr. Frampton-Hair in the morning. Fifty? Ha, I took 150 listens—an overdose of Bob-ituates.

I think it saved me, and I'm not being overly dramatic. I owe that song. I owe the Music Box. I owe rock and roll; it kept me from hurting myself, or worse, doing something to Ilene that would make her scream, and not from a rush of dick, David, and dopamine. Yet, after all that rock music had done for me, I turned my back on it.

The music always healed me. And porn. Porn was another kind of breakup pain medication. One night, after depositing a fistful of tokens into a porn booth near Times Square, I headed a few blocks uptown to see what this bullshit Studio 54 disco thing was all about. I walked along 8th Avenue, mainly because it was cool and dangerous, plus there were a few other notable porn establishments with private booths hungry to suck the coins out of my pocket. I preferred the booths; they had doors that you could close—and lock. The movie theaters were a little too creepy for me. Once your eyes adjusted to the low lighting, you'd scope out your perfect secluded seat at the end of a row and settle in, but inevitably, some man would sit in the seat next to you or just behind you, hoping to get a glimpse or maybe lend a hand. Flickering darkness emboldens perversion.

Sure, the big theaters had some fine, plot-driven, feature-length porn films, usually triple features with a Kung Fu movie mixed in. But way too much unsafe sex was happening in and between and ultimately *on* the seats.

So, whatever you do, stay away from the theaters in the area. Did I mention that Studio 54 used to be a theater?

As I was closing in on 54th Street, I began to hear a swelling chorus of voices. I couldn't make out what they were saying, but there was a buzz of desperation. When I finally arrived at the corner of 54th Street and 8th Avenue and turned that corner to approach the nightclub, the voices and glitz came into tighter focus. I saw couples pleading to gain entry. There were guys from New Jersey with flamboyant shirts begging to be let in. Players from the Dallas Cowboys held their hands aloft in a prayer pose, hoping that a display of god-fearing sensitivity might allow them past the velvet rope.

Nope.

Who got in? Well, it was difficult to determine any real pattern. I could tell you, though, that the real celebrities got inside immediately—almost in a blur—from limo to door in seven seconds flat. As for the civilians, from my vantage point at the perimeter of the disco multitudes, each person's fate was in the hands of this one seemingly apathetic guy holding a clipboard. He was perched on a box. Sometimes he'd stand atop a fire hydrant. He was high above the too-washed masses and yet, he didn't seem to be enjoying the unobstructed view of the pathetic in polyester.

The whole thing seemed so strange to me. As I would soon learn from my father, the scene was like an inversion of the selection process at the Nazi death camps: "Please select me, please, please."

That guy, he had some freaky power—the power to ignore, to make a person feel like a tiny invisible speck of worthless-nothingness-dung. On the surface, he appeared disengaged, but I could see that his eyes were constantly flitting about, discreetly scanning and zeroing in. Although his sense of smell was likely wrecked by various inhaled substances, it was clear he possessed a higher percentage of cone cells than most North American birds of prey. The delicate nocturnal creature atop a box, the man with astonishing night vision, spotted me along the edges. "Back off disco dickface," was the phrase that instantly popped into my mind. His head did a small lift and jerk to the left. Was the Velvet Rope Nazi beckoning me to come inside? He did it again. The head jerk, and this time it was accompanied by a slight, come-right-this-way hand gesture. Me? Disco? Never going to happen. How could a boy mentored by rock legends allow himself to be sullied by the songs of Summer (Donna) and Sunshine (KC and the band).

And then *she* crashes into my mind: Ilene, taker of virginity. Well, you know what? Now I'm going to fuck you in a whole new way. The idea of venturing into the numerically named dance hall would certainly disappoint her and shatter her feelings for me even more. It would make her angry, enraged. Maybe it would hurt her . . .

SCREECHING ROCK AMP FEEDBACK!!!!!!!!!

And there it was, the insane propulsion of breakup revenge, a force that would overtake me and allow Studio 54 to take me into its glittering mirror-ball embrace, past a velvet rope and deep into a cave of the depraved with interior décor inspired by the drug lord, Pablo Escobar, and lighting inspired by Lewis Carroll:

> *"But I don't want to go among mad people," said Alice. "Oh, you can't help that," said the cat. "We're all mad here."*

Rock and roll wept. It was about to lose one of its loyal child soldiers. At that moment, I just didn't care. It was more important to screw over Ilene. I scream. Ilene, I scream your name inside my head. I nodded back to Disco's Decider, the man on the other side of the velvet barbed wire. With a fake ID and genuine Levi's, I was deftly drawn toward an empyrean passageway created by a swift parting of the multicolored bridge and tunnel of bodies.

And so, it was done. I surrendered completely to the throb and the thump of 54. But the Gods of Rock would never stand for such sonic blasphemy. Bracing for the brimstone, I expected their ominous wrath would soon be revealed. They wasted no time. Standing at a long bar fully manned by half-naked men, I became haunted by a vengeful deity who played in the key of G—a smiting beheld through a surplusage of smoke and strobe light.

I rubbed my eyes. I rubbed them again. *No. Dear Rock God, no.*

There, just off to the side, seated in cushioned alcoves, I saw David Bowie swaying to a disco beat. The Vinyl Final Solution had begun.

Electchester Apartments, Queens

LATE 1970s

OTHER THAN AN INDIAN ARROWHEAD, MY FATHER'S FAKE ID WAS ABOUT the oldest thing I had ever held in my hands.

"So, wait . . . wait, I'm trying to understand this; this is a fake document, and Tadeusz Lipski, that's your secret identity?" I asked. This had to be some made up bullshit, something he bought at one of those Times Square stores known for cranking out fake IDs to any kid with a decent weekly allowance. This must've been from the premium collection.

Like Ira Glass narrating *This Eastern European Life*, he began to reveal more parts of his Holocaust story; the rest would slowly drip out over many years. I consider this initial disclosure as the prologue to my father's earlier life, a life story with enough dramatic twists that it could probably be a book. Definitely a decent story for the *Medium* website. Or, at the very least, a blog post on Jewlicious.com.

Some lingering ambiguities were lifted the day he broke his silence. As I came to discover that afternoon, the reason my father made a firm decision not to talk about his past was because he didn't want his sons to be burdened by traumatic memory. He saw what it had done to family friends who survived the war. It's an unfortunate affliction suffered by several second-generation Holocaust survivors. Others, like me—a second gen-er kept in darkness about the terrible past who then has it sprung on them as a young adult—tend to go from zero to wannabe Nazi hunter in sixty seconds. I say "wannabe" because the Simon Wiesenthal Center in Southern California sent back a rather insightful rejection letter when I applied for a position there. Apparently, something about "conspicuous anger issues" disqualified me. In retrospect, it was a wise decision on their part.

Well, if I couldn't search for Nazis, I would research Nazis, settling for total immersion in Holocaust studies. So, in between nights of dancing under a giant coke spoon suspended from on high at Studio 54, I escaped into the dense forest of Holocaust movies and books.

While we're on the topic of books, during my initial genocide fact-finding mission, one of the things that turned up was a beautiful book of photographs by Roman Vishniac. It featured stirring images of Jewish life in Europe before the Nazis rolled in. Many of these photos captured daily rituals in the *shtetl*, depictions of orthodox communities in traditional attire going about their humble lives. I was so excited to give this gift to my father; it was a small gesture of gratitude for sharing his difficult story with me. The reviews are stellar, by the way. Here's a sample pulled from Amazon and GoodReads:

> *"Everyone needs to read this book. I can't believe these photos exist."*
>
> *"A beautiful yet painfully heartbreaking work of photography."*
>
> *"Poignant, historic photographs of Jewish life in Eastern Europe before 1940. I don't think I have ever seen such powerful photographs."*
>
> *"If my parents were alive, I would share it with them. The book is history, art, and vision."*

I remember my gift wrapping—it was craft paper. I felt anything decorative would have been inappropriate. I remember what I wrote on the paper: *Dear Father, I know it has not been easy to talk about your past, but I believe it will have a profound impact on my future. Thanks again. I hope you enjoy these wonderful historic photos.*

"Take it back. Return it to the store. I don't want this crap!" was his unexpected reaction after carefully unwrapping the paper.

"Wait, what? I don't get it. What don't you like about the book? It has all these amazing pictures of life before the war," I responded, attempting to get him to reconsider.

"That's not what we looked like! Not at all," he said in a voice lifting to an alarming volume. "We were assimilated, my family, like a lot of Jews in Warsaw. We were professionals—doctors and business owners. We weren't the religious fanatics who dressed in the black clothes, the *payot*, the hats . . . No, that wasn't us, and you know what? The Germans used that against us in propaganda; it was an easy thing to point out to quickly stir up the hate against us. As if all Jews were like that, like some strange cult. No, take it back. I don't want the book. I don't want to look at those people."

I reluctantly returned it, but part of me wishes I had kept the photo book so that each time I cracked it open I could hear my father's diatribe, like a greeting card, the kind you pry open and hear a tinny version of "Happy Birthday." Only this wouldn't be music, it would be rage against a community of devout ultra-Jews who refused to blend in with the mainstream, whose traditional outward appearance was weaponized and ingeniously used to amplify and normalize the hate.

On second thought, if I did own a copy, I'd toss it into the fireplace. Okay, maybe I wouldn't go as far as book burning. More likely, I'd donate it to a library or stuff it into one of the little free libraries that keep popping up in my neighborhood. Whatever. Just get that mind-fucking, dust-collecting thing off my mental bookshelf.

Berlin, Germany

EARLY 1940s

UNLIKE HIS FATHER, MY FATHER DID NOT ENDURE A BRUTAL TRAIN RIDE TO Treblinka. You need to understand something about Treblinka; it was more sinister than most of the other concentration camps. It was built for a single purpose: death. Men, women, and children arrived, stepped off the train, dropped their belongings, and headed to the gas chambers.

The End.

My father had a different fate. Instead of being counted among the victims of an extremely efficient and industrious extermination system, he became one of the many slave laborers who found themselves embedded into the Make-It-for-Germany factories across Europe. Although not swiftly executed, these war prisoners were slowly worked to death. In some instances, laborers were instantly shredded by British and American fighter planes charged with bombing factories and makeshift hospitals. That is, unless the owner of the building was shrewd enough to paint a red cross on the roof—a vivid deception meant to act as an edifice immunity necklace. Eventually, the Allies caught onto the ersatz Red Cross scam and bombed away.

Spoiler alert: A bomb was dropped onto the factory where my father was sent to produce Marschstiefel, the marching boots worn by German soldiers.

He survived.

What, exactly, were those boots made for? Here's a slight twist on a Nancy Sinatra song to help explain:

> *These boots are made for goose-steppin', and that's just what they'll do, but most of these days these boots are gonna walk all over dead bodies, kick in the doors of Jewish homes, and crush the skulls of terrified Jewish toddlers . . .*

So, how did my father get out of that shitshow? Ladies and gentlemen—*meine Damen und Herren*—let's give a great big round of applause for dysentery.

Chinese Restaurant

FOSTER CITY, CALIFORNIA

WE OPENED OUR MENUS. I LOOKED OUT OVER THE TOP OF PAGE NINE—the thing was thick—and I caught my father's eye. I had questions. There were several blank memory spaces needing to be filled, and the fuzzy stuff needed to be sharpened. And yeah, I know, Holocaust chitchat over a nice birthday dinner might not seem like the finest idea, but I could care less about the best timing when the fact of the matter is, I might not have much time left with the guy. So, I asked again for permission to interrogate, to get things right for the book that I was attempting to write. Pen in one hand, teacup in my other hand, I got ready to take notes.

TODD

My next question, and I admit, probably not the best thing to ask right before a meal, but how long did you work as a slave-laborer in the German boot factory before dysentery sent you to the hospital?

DAD

Seriously? You want to talk about my ass at the dinner table? Okay, sure. But you need to get your facts straight. I didn't make it to the boot factory. I was that sick. Oooh, very bad, very bad, puking from the front and the back. I was a mess. No, I was supposed to work in the boot factory, but thank God I didn't, because otherwise, I wouldn't be here waiting for my wonton soup—and it better be hot.

STEVE

If it's not the temperature of volcanic lava, back to the kitchen it goes.

My father fake stabs Steve with a chopstick.

DAD

Shush, Steve. Yeah, they bombed the boot factory. Nothing left of it—nothing—total rubble. The only reason I survived was because I went from the train station straight to the hospital in Berlin.

TODD

How long were you in the hospital?

DAD

Almost a week. I was crapping that much. And while I was in the hospital . . . boom! A British pilot looking down from the sky hit his target with perfect precision.

Steve interrupts, his hands are in a prayer pose.

STEVE

Thoughts and prayers for all the supple boot leather lost on that tragic day.

I continue taking notes, filling in the details.

TODD

That is . . . certainly . . . news to me . . . Cool. Very cool.

Dad shoots me a look.

TODD

Did I say cool? I mean, whoa, your poor tuchas. Okay, so that's when you're forced into slave labor . . . after you get caught smuggling. But what happened between your arrest and being shipped off to the Make-It-for-Germany boot factory?

My father sighs, calls waiter to table.

DAD

I'll have a Dewars on the rocks. Actually, no ice. Just the scotch.

I'm in a second race against time, and it's causing me all kinds of anxiety. It has nothing to do with finishing this book or getting all the facts straight while my ninety-three-year-old father is alive and kicking and screaming at cable network news. I feel threatened, fearing the opportunity is slipping away, like the walls of other ethnicities are closing in and pushing us aside, making room for their voices, their tragic stories.

Bookshelves which once catered exclusively to our Holocaust—the blockbuster of all Holocausts (we own the copyright and certainly the search engines)—are starting to welcome other genocidal sagas. How long before those memoirs and eyewitness accounts of crimes against humanity crowd us out and become the new mass extermination darlings of independent booksellers. In other words, am I too late to this Holocaust memoir game? Has fatigue around our experience finally set in?

Why do I write so slowly?

Will my father's story, no matter how compelling, be eclipsed by survivor stories from Rwanda, Vietnam, Mozambique, Syria, or Darfur? I mean, George Clooney was all over Darfur, and sure, things have been quiet lately. Perhaps he's focusing more on child labor issues in the chocolate and coffee industries, but come on, how do you compete against that Clooney awareness bump?

DOCTOR'S NOTE

Please excuse Todd's fears and apprehensions. Our research shows that descendants of people who survived the Holocaust have different stress hormone profiles than their peers, perhaps predisposing them to anxiety disorders.

—Yours truly,
Dr. Yehuda and the team
at the Icahn School of Medicine

Warsaw, Poland

EARLY 1930s

THE POLICE CAPTAIN WHO ISSUED MY FATHER'S FALSE IDENTITY PAPERS would often patrol the area near the final trolley car stop. Seeing him was a huge comfort because it was always assumed that if an arrest did occur, he'd use his rank to intervene and shield my father from the Gestapo, many of whom spent their time on patrol casually standing around smoking cigarettes with other Gestapo guys. You know, just shooting the shit instead of shooting Jews.

But on this day in the fall, an exact day and date that my father couldn't recall, something was off; the vibe was peculiar. He stepped off the trolley car and saw the police captain, but this time, he failed to beam the "all-clear" smile to my father. Instead, his eyes widened, which was followed by a barely perceptible head-shaking gesture; he was covertly communicating a distress signal. With more and more reports about smugglers, mostly coming from Poles eager to turn in Jews, the Gestapo was given strict orders to put the kibosh on all black-marketeering activities.

He didn't see it coming. A hand sheathed in black leather grabbed my father by his collar. Further up the body from that clenched fist was a hostile mouth. And just like in so many Holocaust movies . . .

"PAPERS!" it sternly shouted.

After examining the perfectly forged document, the raging mouth spit out a few questions:

"What do you have?" "What are you hiding?" "Are you a Jew?"

My father answered: "Medicines. That's what I have now. Sometimes I get meats or bread. I make money off the dirty Jews."

Those were the last words he spoke before being brutally thrown into a truck with other smugglers and taken to the Gestapo headquarters. He wished three other words that were trapped inside of him could have been released, carried upon a stream of air until they reached his home, landing gently in the room where his father sat waiting for his return. The words "I'll be okay" would remain outside of the Ghetto wall, tightly sealed behind his quivering lips.

On that day, the sky collapsed upon the young smuggler.

It was the last day he would ever see his father.

The last time he saw his mother had been three weeks earlier. Like many residents in the Ghetto, she became quite ill. Fortunately, she had connections: a husband who could admit her into a hospital. Unfortunately, the Nazis went through hospitals with guns blazing and shot up most of the patients. After all, why waste good medicines on sick Jews? In fact, a scene in *Schindler's List* illustrated the fate of Jews in Ghetto hospitals so perfectly, that when I saw the film with my father, he lurched forward from his theater seat and cried out, "Mama!" He slowly migrated back into his original viewing position. My eyebrows instantly arched to new heights on my forehead. I delicately placed the extra-large bucket of popcorn onto the floor and discreetly shoved it far back under the seat. No way I could eat another kernel after that outburst. My eyebrows remained locked in that severe Joan Crawford position for at least fifteen seconds.

There is a tarnished silver lining: a bullet to the chest in a hospital bed meant that my grandmother, Teofila, was not sent to Treblinka; she could have a proper burial in the Jewish Cemetery in Warsaw. The Kaddish prayer could be recited. There was time for mourning.

Over the years, I've made three visits to the desecrated cemetery in search of my grandmother's grave site. Once with my father and brother, once with my partner, Diana, and once with my daughter, Lauren. I haven't found it yet, but I'll keep looking. Maybe I'll have better luck when I finally take my son, Reid. You know Reid, he's the kid who slept on the dog bed at my post-divorce house. He's a great scout and retriever.

Warsaw to Berlin

EARLY 1940s

DAVID DIAMENTSTEIN—OOPS, SCRATCH THAT—TADEUSZ LIPSKI, WAS apprehended near the Ghetto wall. Since he was a "Christian" smuggler looking to take advantage of desperate Jews, he was not placed in a concentration camp. Instead, he was drafted to support the German war effort.

Before being transported to a Berlin boot factory, this twelve-year-old Jew—I mean, "Christian" boy—was tossed into a truck with several other smugglers and taken to Gestapo headquarters, which was now housed in the Warsaw post office. It was a cold, cavernous structure. Nazi flags hanging throughout the building created a fascist-fabulous ambience. Not surprisingly, it had become the latest design trend across occupied Europe.

After taking in the sea of swastikas, the next thing my father noticed was the extremely long line of people waiting for their physical exams. After all, the Germans wanted able bodies that would not easily succumb to the brutalities and stresses inside their factories—conditions which make Foxconn manufacturing facilities seem like a Sandals resort. The German doctors checked for the usual medical suspects: head lice, respiratory illness, hernia. *HERNIA*? That would mean drop your drawers and expose your penis, and if that penis was circumcised, it would fuck you so hard it would kill you.

What's a Jew masquerading as a Christian supposed to do in this situation? Take a piss, that's what. And not in your pants, although he was certainly scared enough to let loose in his only pair of trousers—the one with a hidden pocket. He stepped out of the long line to relieve his full bladder, waited in the bathroom for a few extra minutes, then returned to the end of the line. It was now even longer. This is when survival game theory kicked in. My father's strategy was based on keen observation; it didn't require the brains of Edward Teller to see the logic: extract yourself from the examination line. Go to the bathroom. Wait. Torture your penis in an effort to reverse your circumcision. Return to the back of the line.

He performed this slick routine two more times. When he finally reached the front of the line, the doctors were understandably exhausted and therefore far less thorough in their poking, grabbing, and cavity explorations. In the interest of time, they checked my father's head, his mouth, and ears; they also listened to his chest. His testicles remained in hiding. Healthy enough to report for slave labor duties, my father's next excursion was a train ride from Warsaw to a boot factory just outside of Berlin.

Was it the bacteria aboard the train that caused his intestines to inflame? Did a feculent bowl attack his bowels? Maybe his stomach went haywire due to the meager portion of rancid mystery slop? Whatever the reason, a serious case of dysentery sent him directly to the nearby hospital as soon as he arrived in Berlin. Two days later, the factory, and many of the workers inside of it, ceased to exist.

Chinese Restaurant

FOSTER CITY, CALIFORNIA

WAITER PLACES ANOTHER ORDER OF EGG ROLLS ON OUR TABLE. PERFECT timing for a schlong-shaped appetizer considering where the conversation is heading. The only food more appropriate (in shape and allergens) would be the geoduck clam.

DAD

Well, you know what I always told you guys, your dicks will get you into trouble, and boy did they ever . . . hooo, I could write my own book about that. As for my putz? Mine nearly killed me. A few times.

TODD

(sarcastically)
Right, your accursed circumcision; the "cut Diamond . . . "

STEVE

(snarky) The "snipped Lipski . . . "

TODD

The "severed Diamentstein . . . "

DAVE

How about we lacerate this part of the conversation?

Steve holds up his index finger.

STEVE

Fine. Okay, so to recap . . . number one: Going number one saved your life.

Steve then holds up two fingers.

STEVE

Number two: Going number two saved your life.

I shake my head at the scatological references,
although, if you think about it . . .

STEVE

I know you have more questions, Todd, but can we hang on Dad's testicles for a moment longer?

TODD

Ha, you mean Dad's shellfish allegory story?

STEVE

Uh . . . no. I mean Dad's shellfish *allergy* story. Jeez, you been writing much?

I laugh, rub my temples.

TODD

Maybe not enough . . .

My father tries to break up the testes talk, makes a cross with his chopsticks.

DAD

Great, terrific. First my ass, now my balls?

Steve fake gestures reaching out to waiter.

STEVE

Hey Todd, can someone call the waiter over, I'd like to put in an order for shrimp with lobster-crab-mussel-and-oyster sauce.

DAD

Well, how about that . . . my sons trying to finish what the Nazis started.

TODD

I don't know, Dad. It was pretty scary. I was what, like ten? The pounding on the front door, Mom opening it to see you leaning on a taxi driver for support. You were screaming from the pain. Mom walked you to the sofa, laid you down, and pulled off your pants.

Steve holds out his hands, makes a large circle the size of a basketball.

STEVE

It was like someone took a bike pump, shoved the needle into your balls, and pumped them up, but in the middle of inflating, got distracted and went waaaay past the recommended PSI.

We all laugh at Steve's comment.

TODD

Right, Steve, but Mom was cool. I expected her to freak out or cry hysterically. Instead, she put her hands on her hips in that movie starlet way and said, "Ooooooh Dave, please don't change, I like 'em like that."

DAD

(attempts to change subject)
Yeah, yeah. And then Dr. Ross came to the apartment, gave me a shot, and the whole situation was deflated. Now, can one of you jokers pass me the tea?

I return to my notebook.

TODD

Okay, okay. But let's get back to Berlin. So, no boot factory. But how long after being released from the hospital until you get to your slave-labor gig?

My father spoons more food onto his plate while answering.

DAD

Immediately. And I guess Nazis liked milk with their cookies because I was put on a train and sent to work on a dairy farm.

TODD

In Baldenburg, right?

DAD

No. The train took me to Baldenburg. I was picked up at the station by a farmer. His name was Schtach, a sadistic son of a bitch. He brought me to his farm to work. It was in a rural village called Schlochau.

I quickly write that fact in my notebook.

TODD

Great, wow, that's the first time you ever mentioned his name.

DAD

Yeah, well . . . maybe that's because the bastard beat me. Every day another beating. The only thing that made it tolerable was that—and I never told you this—while living there, I lost my virginity to a farmer's daughter.

Waiter places pork dumplings on the table, hears the virginity comment, smiles.

WAITER

Here's your pork dumplings. The rest of the food will be coming out shortly.

Steve can't resist the opening.

STEVE

Oh, thank you, God of segues! Now what were you saying about porking a farmer's daughter?

I'm amazed at hearing this.

TODD

How old were you? How old was the farmer's daughter?

DAD

Hmm, I was thirteen—

Steve nearly chokes on a dumpling.

STEVE

Thirteen? Whoa. 'Today I am a man'—that's some special bar mitzvah gift. What'd we get? Oh, right, a frickin' savings bond.

DAD

(sardonically)

Aww, *bubbeleh* . . . My heart bleeds for you, you poor unfortunate street urchins with your fancy bar mitzvah parties. Oh, I'm sorry, were the tuxedos not to your liking? You know what I got when I turned thirteen? A Beat Mitzvah.

Steve pouts like a brat, reflecting on his bar mitzvah day humiliation.

STEVE

Boo-hoo. Well, it beats mangling your haftorah in front of 150 judgy, scowling Jews. PTHD. Post Traumatic—

My father finishes Steve's sentence, having heard it a million and thirteen times before.

DAD

Haftorah Disorder. Yeah, yeah, I get it. We were surprised you didn't run away to the Midwest, become a gentile, and live off pastrami sandwiches on white bread. I heard that after your botched performance, guests ripped up their original checks and wrote new ones for much smaller amounts.

I continue riffing with my father.

TODD

I think you made the rabbi cry.

DAD

Yeah, he was about to give Steve the bar mitzvah blessing but changed his mind after that incredible Torah mangling. Oy, and remember how he shocked the congregation? How the rabbi angrily turned away from you, kicked over the pulpit, and stormed off the Bimah?

TODD

Oh, and the poor Haftorah tutor . . . The temple confiscated his teaching license, right Dad?

DAD

Ach, what a pity. Such a nice man.

STEVE

You guys done with the roast yet?

DAD

Mmmm, yes, kiddo. I'd say the roast was . . . pretty well done.

I give a hearty thumbs up.

TODD

Nailed the dad joke, Dad.

My brother finds his opening and chimes in.

STEVE

Speaking of nailing, I gotta ask you, Dad, how old was the girl who took your virginity?

DAD

Eva? She was twenty-six, maybe twenty-seven.

I drop my chopsticks. Steve spits out his tea. My father ignores the shock of his sons, offers up the reality of the situation.

DAD

Now before you think, 'Oh yeah, serves you right, Schtach, you ruthless German bastard. A Jew violated your *shiksa* daughter with a circumcised penis,' my virginity snatcher was indeed the daughter of a farmer, but one who lived down the road, not under the same leaking roof. Ooh, she was a sexy tomato, *zaftig*, big . . .

My father puts his hands in front of his chest and squeezes.

STEVE

(incredulous, but giddy)
Dad, did you just call that woman a vegetable? Hmm, or is it a fruit?

I push for additional details.

TODD

Whoa, whoa, whoa. I'm more interested in her age than her home address and measurements. I mean, having sex with her, wasn't that statutory—

Steve interrupts; he can't resist.

STEVE

Hold on, twenty-six? Did you say she was a farm girl or a schoolteacher from Florida?

My father cuts off his sons.

DAD

Nah, nah, no one thought like that, not where I was forced to live, and certainly not during wartime. However, having sex with this woman, it could have killed me, you know.

STEVE

Down-on-the-farm asphyxiation . . . is that your kink, Dad? Nice.

My father brushes off Steve's snide comment.

DAD

Oooh, I was super horny back then. We'd shtup in the morning and again in the late afternoon. I committed a crime twice a day, because in the eyes of the German government, her baby-making parts were pure Aryan, and anyone other than a pure Aryan who dared to penetrate a fraulein could be arrested or put to death.

Steve seems to be holding onto an earlier comment, sees a chance to joke about it.

STEVE

Harsh. But wait a sec, can we rewind to the "lycopening" of women. Dad, let's try this . . . I'll give you the name of a celebrity or friend of the family, and you say the variety of tomato that pops into your head.

DAD

G'head, give it your best shot.

STEVE

Jennifer Lopez.

DAD

Ooh, she's a spicy tomato.

I shake my head, amused.

STEVE

Lainie Kazan. You love Lainie Kazan.

DAD

Now that's a juicy tomato.

STEVE

Mrs. Collins.

DAD

The neighbor? The one with the big . . . ? Oh, a hot . . . hot tomato.

STEVE

Mom.

My father gets a little choked up.

DAD

The sweetest, most gorgeous tomato.

Now I jump into the game.

TODD

Okay . . . Rivka, the soldier who fought with you in Israel. By the way, did the two of you make us a sister we don't know about?

He suddenly gets sharp with me.

DAD

Why are you such a putz. You don't mess with Rivka. Fierce soldier, that one. A killer, literally. She could murder you with her bare hands.

STEVE

So . . . a slightly bitter tomato?

I seize the moment, hoping to get more details about a topic he rarely discusses: his time in Israel.

TODD

Since you bring up the killer tomato, I have some questions about that, too, Dad. About the war in Israel, but I'll ask you later . . . that okay?

DAD

Maybe. Not sure I want to get into all that. And if you even start to lecture me about the apartheid bullshit . . .

TODD

I won't . . . well . . . I'll really try not to.

I take a sip of tea. It's cold. My father takes a long sip of his scotch.

Earth

1860–OCTOBER 7, 2023

Want to hear some more shit? I came upon it while doing research for my father's story. It's the approximate death count of global conflicts and genocides that occurred during the period between America's Civil War and a recent barbaric assault on a portion of holy land tucked between a river and a sea.

When you factor in civilians, military personnel, and indirect deaths through disease, starvation, and violence, you're looking at hundreds of millions of deaths (plus 1,200 on October 7, 2023, plus legitimate retributive justice in the thousands that followed).

That's more than 5,000 Vietnam Veterans Memorials. You think the Oscars In-Memoriam section is overly long? Imagine an In-Memoriam that listed each of the conflicts (and their respective death tolls). Good luck getting Sarah McLachlan or any unionized musicians to sign up for that interminable gig.

This is what I'm talking about, and it's what I could be up against. To have even the slightest chance of sharing my family's Holocaust story in published form before my father checks out, these other grisly events need to remain mere footnotes in history, not emotionally-wrenching personal accounts that receive magniloquent reviews by Amazon Prime members and Oprah.

There are millions of stories about lives lost to war and savagery since the mid-nineteenth century. It's a staggering body count. If even the smallest fraction of these first, second, or third generation survivors get their shit together and crank out a memoir or novel, my chances diminish further; although, to be honest, I'm not too worried about losing mindshare to the Armenian experience. You see, even though they kicked off genocide in the twentieth century, they've received little recognition for the oppression.

Elizabeth, a writer and friend who works at Ancestry.com, validated this literary void (*Black Dog of Fate* being a notable exception). Her people are Armenian, plus she knows a thing or two about family history.

But who knows, with all the new streaming services looking for content, not to mention the fact that Elizabeth is a heck of a writer, maybe Armenia will get a shot and successfully suck up more of the atrocity oxygen.

Gasp.

Schlochau, Germany

EARLY 1940s

EVEN THOUGH A LOT OF CHEAP LABOR AND HIGH-QUALITY LEATHER WAS blown away in the boot factory bombing, the Germans still had a few bodies they could snatch from hospitals for reassignment to the Aryan cause.

Barely recovered from his bout with dysentery, my father was placed on a train to Baldenburg. Upon his arrival, he was picked up at the station by Farmer Schtach and quickly put to strenuous work in the remote village of Schlochau. This Warsaw Ghetto city kid was about to become a country boy whether he liked it or not.

The farmer called my father Hans. He couldn't bring himself to use a low-bred Polish name when spewing orders at his child detainee, so Hans it would be. First it was David. Then Tadeusz. And now, Hans. That's a lot of names—nowhere near Kanye-level, of course: Kanye, Ye, Yeezy, Yeezus, Dr. West, YeNazi, Christian Genius Billionaire Kanye West—still, it's a wonder that I don't have to devote several pages of this book to an identity crisis.

It was the standard slave labor on a German farm routine:

My father would wake up in a small attic room on a bed made of straw, nudged out of bed by a herding dog. He'd eat porridge with a slice of a stale bread and wash it down with a cup of lukewarm tea. A hard slap across the face started the day, and another came before he was shoved out the door.

Feed hay and water to the cows, clean their crap, and put it aside to use as fertilizer. Groom the horses and feed them mashed potatoes. Go back and milk the cows. Get punched in the ear and stomach by an irate farmer. Harvest wheat, bundle it, stand it up to dry. Pick vegetables. Clean the stables. Take cows to the field. Have sex in a forest with a zaftig farmer's daughter. Get back to work. Get hit across the thigh and shoulder and neck with a riding crop. Absorb harsh verbal abuse from farmer's wife. Have sex again in the forest with farmer's daughter. Head back to the house. Have supper. Get thrown to the ground and stomped on. Repeatedly. Climb upstairs to your small attic room. Hear the door lock. Cry. Sleep. Rise and shine and do it all over again and again for more than two years.

My father endured the daily mistreatment and toughed out the constant physical beatings for way longer than either of his sons would last; heck, after a single day of slave life on the farm, we'd have thrown ourselves to the wolves or the trackers who patrolled the forests in search of escapees.

On the other hand, there were those literal rolls in the hay with a sheep-herding older seductress. Sometimes twice a day, and that almost made slave-farm living worth living for.

Chinese Restaurant

FOSTER CITY, CALIFORNIA

JOHN DEWAR & SONS MUST BE LOOKING DOWN ON US FROM HEAVEN because our waiter appears just as my father drains his glass.

WAITER

Another Dewars, Mr. Diamond?

My father nods vigorously.

DAD

I'd say bring the bottle, but let's just start by refilling this glass.

Steve lightheartedly goads him.

STEVE

You know, while we're on the topic of beatings, did Dad ever hit you, Todd? I know I got 'the belt' a few times.

My father shakes his head, denying the accusation.

DAD

Never raised a hand to either of my sons.

STEVE

Oooh, I see what you did there, 'never raised a hand.' Nice. You found a 'belt loophole' with that statement.

I join in, challenging my father's statement.

TODD

Oh yeah you did. I'll never forget being on the receiving end of your holiday rage, Dad.

DAD

Whaddaya talking about?

TODD

Let's see . . . okay, I was fifteen. I spent my weekly allowance prematurely with Johnny, the new weed dealer at the school. He was selling dime bags—all buds, by the way, and not the usual buds, twigs, and seeds.

Steve pats me on the back.

STEVE

Good for you, Todd, supporting a disruptive start-up.

TODD

Thanks, Steve. I asked for an advance—I called it a Christmas bonus. Dad, you were on the sofa, reading the *Long Island Press*, so I couldn't see your face. But from behind the headlines, I heard you say, "NO, I'm not made of money!" So, I just walked away, but under my breath I said 'Scrooge.' Perfect holiday season burn, right?

Steve punches the air.

STEVE

Hey, Papa Tyson, you tracking with this?

My father facetiously fiddles with his hearing aid.

DAD

Darn, need to change the battery in this thing . . . you say something?

TODD

Yup, right response. Because you heard something different. You thought I said, 'Screw you!' Oh man, were you furious. You threw down the paper and screamed, 'HOW DARE YOU SAY "SCREW YOU" TO YOUR FATHER.'

STEVE

Oh no, Todd. So, belt or back of hand?

TODD

A fist. Right to my chest. Lifted me off the ground and sent me hurtling backwards; I'm a high-speed projectile stopped by a collision with a closet door in the dining room. Which collapsed.

Steve performs rapid air karate chops.

STEVE

Where was Mom during Dad's best Bruce Lee imitation?

TODD

Well, after hearing the crash, Mom bolted out of the kitchen, quickly analyzed the situation, grabbed the *Long Island Press*, and started swatting us with the rolled-up pages.

Steve feigns shock. Fans himself with napkin.

STEVE

No! Were you having farm flashbacks, Dad? Did you suddenly picture Mom in overalls holding a wooden spoon, a whip, a pitchfork?

TODD

Bro, it was rough at first, but then Dad and I started cracking up, because as we took the beating from Mom, he looked at me and said, "Hey, Todd, we're like an Italian family. From New Jersey."

My father lifts his fist to his mouth and blows on it like a gunslinger.

Summer Camp, Winsted, Connecticut

MID-1970s

LIKE FATHER (AND FARMER'S DAUGHTER), LIKE SON (AND FARMER'S daughter). The difference is that my experience was less a roll in the hay and more a pitchfork into the penis.

I'll begin this down-on-the-farm story by saying that basketball is a game of hands. You dribble the ball with one hand; you switch the ball between left and right hand; you arc the ball with your fingertips and wrist and set it on a course to circles made of metal.

Basketball is also a game of feet. You walk as you dribble the basketball; you run down the court to receive a pass; you pivot; you jump and land hard after going up for a rebound. And, as I would discover one summer far away from the metal backboards in Queens, basketball is also a game of penis. Here's the thing: if you hurt your penis, you can't really run. Think about it—a sore penis, pressing against briefs that are pressing against tight shorts. Tight shorts from the seventies, no less.

Technically, I didn't hurt the thing; she did.

Who's *she*? A lovely girl who lived down the road at a farmhouse close to the camp. We met at a Friendly's Ice Cream restaurant in town. I can't mention any names because the woman who shook my reproductive organ the night before the big game against Camp Firebird—and nearly dismembered it in the process—grew up to be a mover and shaker in the nonprofit world, delivering healthcare to West African countries.

Please excuse the mixed sports metaphors, but this third-base event came back to bite me on the ass. No, her teeth were not involved. It was a hand job and only a hand job—the very first hand job ever provided by a hand other than my own. I wished other parts of her anatomy were involved, but it was not happening, not this summer.

There was this one moment during her piston-like back-and-forth technique when I noticed her tongue slip out of her mouth, the way a child's does when they are concentrating hard to color inside the lines. The instant I saw that moist little tongue poke out, I thought, *Hmm, maybe if I ask just the right way, those taste buds might replace her fist of fury . . .*

I was too scared to ask. She kept up her bold, resolute strokes. Hard grip, hard everything. It felt like I was in the hands of a Soviet-era tug-of-war champion. Electrodes inside my urethra would have felt slightly better. I took another peek at her tongue and thought, *At this point, I don't even want a blow job—what I want more than anything is for that tongue to lick the wound that is quickly forming on my penis.* There was only one way to bring this turbulent Tilt-A-Ween ride to a stop. *Okay, here we go; open wide pretty wildflowers resting at my feet under a starry Connecticut night sky; you are about to be fertilized.*

I liked the farmer's daughter. She was different than the other girls at my camp. For starters, she was not Jewish. This fairer maiden was smart, more radical. Her deeply curious mind made me think about things like politics, feminism, art, and composting. But I was smack in the middle of my Duh-nder Years, and I couldn't quite express my gratitude in spoken words or mushy love letters. I did, however, find a way to let her know what I was feeling: I used my hands.

See, I could sense that she held some insecurity about her hair and glasses, so the few times we made out, I would gently glide my hand from the top of her hair to the place just behind her ear where the temples of her glasses rested. Then, I would slowly drag my finger across the temple till it reached the lens frame. With tremendous restraint and patience, I'd trace the lens frame with my finger, and when I finally reached her nose, I'd poke it. Twice. That made her laugh. It made me feel pretty good as well.

The morning after my farmhandjob, I awoke with severely marred morning wood. There was no way I could play in the basketball game. Impossible. I could barely walk from my bed to the bathroom. Fortunately, my counselor Glen was cool. He had long blond hair, leather bracelets, and a pierced ear. He'd be sympathetic. Plus, he played piano. The guy was a living, breathing mix tape, featuring songs by Stevie Wonder, Billy Joel, Elton John, and Joni Mitchell. I told Glen the truth about why I wasn't up for playing, but without revealing the hand behind it.

I was certain he'd keep the secret of my sore penis and even concoct a believable excuse on my behalf for having to sit out such a crucial game. I was embarrassed. I let my team down. Glen put a comforting arm around my shoulder and said, "Thanks, for telling me. It's fine. Now let's tell the other guys."

What a guy.

Amidst the chaos of suiting up for the game, Glen told the team he had an announcement. "Listen up, gentlemen, no Diamond in the game today. Andy, you'll be playing forward. You know why? Because this selfish asshole got himself an oozing lesion on his dick. Apparently, someone gave him a hand job with a sandpaper glove."

Immediately, all kinds of stuff came flying at my head: towels, deodorant cans, sneakers. They all asked who had done the debilitating deed. I refused to give up her name.

And, of course, they demanded to see my dick. I stood my ground and refused to show it. But I lost that battle. Unlike my father, whose penis remained hidden at a critical moment, mine was forced out into the open.

I can't stop thinking about just how many ground-breaking literary talents might emerge from the ashes of the inhumanity and suffering listed a few pages back. New voices that will be proclaimed as this generation's Eli Wiesel or the next Viktor Frankl. Brilliant and important voices from cutting edge Hells, making profound contributions to catastrophe documentation.

I feel it in my gut—somewhere out there, probably in an attic, there's the hidden diary of a young Rohingya girl; it is heartbreaking, and it is unfinished. Of course.

Is this what consumers of the genocide genre will desire next? How do you get your story heard in the post-Holocaust Holocaust era? And what about the literary agents and publishers? If a few of the modern mass-execution stories start trending, then naturally, that's where most book deals will flow. Those of us vying for a few inches of space on "Holocaust Studies" bookshelves, or a place buried deep within the algorithmic layers on Amazon, will have to duke it out for remaining scraps. Or simply surrender and climb aboard the cattle car on a journey to self-publishing.

Schlochau, Germany

MID-1940s

ONE DAY, WHILE HE WAS OUT IN THE PASTURE, PROBABLY MIDWAY through his internee duties, a slow-rolling army tank formation approached the farm. Leading the tanks was a uniformed soldier on horseback. The soldier dismounted.

My father immediately took flight, but the soldier shouted, ordering him to STOP! My father heard the command, but oddly, it wasn't the language he expected. He thought the last word he'd hear prior to taking a bullet in the back would have been HALT! That's what a German soldier would have hollered to a fleeing "Polish-Christian" farm slave. The word JUDE! would've followed HALT! had the soldier known about the kind of penis that was administering the twice-daily shtupings to the off-limits *Volksdeutsche* private parts that were tutoring my father in the ways of *geschlechtsverkehr* (it's a German word for sex, but it sure sounds like an onomatopoeia to me).

Fearing that this was the end, he HALTED, put both hands above his head, turned slowly, and warily walked toward the soldier. *At least I won't die a virgin* was one of the first things that popped into his mind as he approached the man about to shoot him.

Of the five shots fired that afternoon on a farm in rural Germany, not a single bullet went through my father.

"HALT! HALT! *OSTANOVKA!*"

The soldier who'd commanded him to STOP! spoke a lot of Russian, a little Polish, and a little German. My father spoke a lot of Polish, a little German, and a bit of Russian. It's a bit confusing, but now imagine how much it boggled my father's mind when he saw the star of David dangling from a gold chain around the soldier's neck. At first, he thought it was a trick, a Jew honeypot. He stayed silent for a long time, shrouding his past, withholding any information that might expedite the release of a bullet from its chamber.

The soldier reached into his pocket and said: "*Nimm es . . .* "

"*Voz'mi eto . . . Weź to . . .* "

In other words, "Take it."

Upon hearing Polish, my father reached out to accept the candy. He quickly devoured it. The soldier gave him another piece. He could see the large bruises on my father's face and body.

"Name. What is your name, child?" he inquired.

"Tadeusz. Tadeusz Lipski," my father responded hesitantly.

"So, you're Polish . . . Do they hit you, Tadeusz? Do they beat you?"

My father didn't answer at first; he just looked to the ground, afraid to make eye contact with the soldier.

He tried again, "Please, Tadeusz, answer me. Do they beat you?"

My father nodded slowly. The Russian soldier then got down on one knee, looked straight into my father's eyes, and asked, "Are you a Jew?"

Panic. My father looked up to the sky, seeking guidance from his mother . . . and God. Given the slow prayer-connection speeds out there on the farm, his missing-in-action God and dead parent do not receive the message; he'd have to make this decision on his own.

My father squeezed his eyes hard, bracing for the bullet. "Yes, I am a Jew, yes."

The soldier brought the boy's head into his chest, offering a brief moment of comfort and assurance. He stood up, adjusted his cap, and placed a hand on his pistol.

"Tadeusz, I am also a Jew."

My father took a deep, shuddering breath.

The soldier spoke firmly, "Wait here. Do not move. Do you understand? Stay right here."

The Russian soldier walked to the farmhouse; it was a good distance away. My father collapsed to the ground, pulled his knees up to his chest, and did exactly as he was told. He watched the soldier walk away, his speed increasing as he approached the house. He entered through the open front door; he closed it behind him.

Two shots.

My father flinched and pressed his body more tightly into the ground.

There was a long pause. Two more shots fired. A brief pause.

Another loud bang.

There were now five less bullets in the war. The soldier emerged from the house.

He did not close the door behind him.

Schlochau, Germany

MID-1940s

ALL ABOARD. IT'S YET ANOTHER TRAIN RIDE FOR MY FATHER. THIS TIME, A one-way trip to . . . Go ahead, take a wild guess. If you answered Dachau—an obvious choice due to its proximity to the farm and a place of slavery and emancipation—you'd be dead wrong.

Bergen-Belsen? Nope, you're cold.
Ravensbruck?
You're getting warmer.
Sobibor?
Colder.
Majdanek?
Nah, colder.
Chelmno?
Colder.
Auschwitz. Has to be Auschwitz.
Much, much warmer.
Got it! Treblinka, of course.
No, but definitely warmer.
Belzec?

Oh hot, very hot.

So, Belzec?

No, not Belzec.

Warsaw, actually. And then onto Lodz. Belzec was a headstone's throw away, but by the time my father arrived in Lodz, the camps had already been liberated. Just like him.

After unloading his gun into the Schtach family, the Russian soldier walked directly up to my father. He put one hand on his gun. With his other hand, he reached for my father's shoulder and pressed it firmly, assuring him that he was safe and he would be sent back to Poland to look for any surviving members of his family. The kid was stunned, certain he'd be receiving the sixth bullet of the afternoon. Or the consolation prize of being sent to a concentration camp.

My father did not break down in tears. There was no show of emotion. He'd buried that kind of thing long ago. He just took a long breath and reached out to shake the soldier's hand.

It was an unusual sensation—a man's hand that wasn't being forcefully thrown into his body. Eventually, the soldier released his hand from my father's powerful grip of gratitude. Farming in Germany makes you uber strong . . . and calloused. The liberator delivered a brief lecture, including a few pearls of Russian paternal advice like eat more *borscht* (but go easy on the sour cream) and, "Now do you appreciate a Soviet winter?" He also imparted stern warnings about post-war dangers, and there were plenty. The world at that time was precarious; a slight populist breeze would be enough to reignite the underlying antisemitism.

"But I need to go back into the house to get my things," my father pleaded.

"You can't. I'm sorry, I will not allow it," replied the soldier. He was being protective.

In the Warsaw Ghetto, it was not uncommon to walk among the dead. It's something you got used to; the bodies were everywhere. At what point, though, did my father and his father become so numb to stepping around the corpses?

Remarkably, they learned to live with death. It was just part of tough city life. Perhaps things would have been different if the Ghetto had a Mayor Giulianski in charge—then those bodies might not have piled up, and if there was a Yiddish smut theater in Midtown, it'd be shuttered tight.

My father kept insisting that going back into the house would not disturb him in the least. He could handle a midday stroll among the corpses; he had experience. He was fortified. Crime scenes against humanity, even ones that featured multiple chalk outlines, would not make him recoil. He was detached, cool, and inured; he could land a supporting role as the new rookie kid on *CSI: Warsaw Ghetto.*

But the Russian soldier refused to allow him back inside. Besides, it wasn't necessary. Because in addition to his freedom, the soldier gave my father something far more valuable than his meager possessions: a wad of money—enough to buy food, clothing, and supplies for several weeks after making the journey back to Warsaw.

Okay, then, here we go again, David-Tadeusz-Hans. Grab a seat. You're taking another train ride. All aboard to Warsaw. Well, not exactly aboard. Trains were packed after the war; there were so few of them running. Yet somehow, he snagged a seat with an absolutely unobstructed view of the countryside. One potential problem: if he sat upright or lifted his head up too far from the roof of the train where he was pressed face down—and holding on for dear life—that head might be lopped off instantly by an unforeseen tunnel entrance.

The soldier cautioned him that riding inside the train would be too dangerous, especially if he was outed as a Jew. Trains at the time were often filled with soldiers who were not feeling the love for Jews. They believed Jews had dragged them into the fight and were primarily responsible for the misery and suffering of everyone who wasn't a

Jew. Also, and this is perhaps the most significant reason for imperilment, Poles were deeply concerned about survivors returning to towns and cities to reclaim their properties. Like wolfish hermit crabs, the vacated homes were quickly inhabited by Poles during the period of mass incarceration.

Chinese Restaurant

FOSTER CITY, CALIFORNIA

Steve speaks loudly and excitedly;
others overhear his questions.

STEVE

Are you fucking kidding me? After all that, the Russian soldier then puts you on top of a train?! Berlin to Warsaw on top—not inside—a train?

I'm writing furiously in my notebook.

TODD

That is some Tom Cruise shit, Dad. You never told us that.

DAD

Tell 'em two things, hold back one.

I respond while still writing notes.

TODD

You learn that in Israel, while drinking the milk-and-honey Kool-Aid?

My brother wants more of the story.

STEVE

Can we get back to *Yiddish Impossible* starring Dave Cruiski?

DAD

Wow, you're all hopped up on oolong, aren't you, Son? So, look, Europe was raw after the war. Cities were smoldering. And Gentiles . . . well, they weren't exactly planning parades for returning Jews.

TODD

Well, at least you had a seat with a nice view.

So, I have a theory, and I don't think any global economist or Holocaust scholar would back me up on it, but the way I see it, the extermination of Jews was basically a fundamental part of Hitler's economic stimulus program. The Fuhrer's "Make Germany Great Again" platform promised economic prosperity coupled with the restoration of a once-glorious national dignity. Cool, I get that. It's a powerful populist promise. But this is what I believe might have gone down in planning sessions that were held behind closed doors.

And since I'm not pursuing the Hannah Arendt Prize for Political Thought, I will be channeling Mel Brooks and early Woody Allen to help explain the banality behind such evil. And yes, of course I realize I am punching way above my satirist weight:

> *Hermann Göring and a group of economic ministers are meeting in a conference room to discuss plans for Germany's national restoration initiative. The ministers rise to their feet and give the Sieg Heil salute when Göring enters the room.*

GÖRING

Guten morgen, economic ministers. Please sit, sit. Now then, let's start today's meeting with your economic recovery plan. May I see it?

Unprepared, the ministers scramble about, opening their briefcases, looking under the conference room table, patting down their freshly pressed uniform pockets. Hermann Göring is clearly irritated as he observes the scene through tightly pressed fingertips, a classic evil-mastermind-of-the-master-race pose.

MINISTERS

Um, jawohl, Reichsmarschall Göring. It's got to be here somewhere. Now where did we put das protokoll. Hmm, maybe the German Shepard ate it?

The Nazi dad joke falls flat. Göring is not amused. The ministers stifle their laughter.

GÖRING

Achhhh!

MINISTERS

Das tut mir leid! Sorry, so sorry.

GÖRING

Give me some chalk. I'm going to the blackboard.

MINISTERS

Your Venn diagrams are wunderbar, Herr Göring.

GÖRING

Danke schon. Now pay close attention. You all know Reich Minister of Economics, Hjalmar Schacht?

MINISTERS

Ya, ya.

GÖRING

Well, we've been brainstorming, and we feel it is impossible to simply grow ourselves out of this depression. However, we can quickly TAKE our way out of this never-ending economic slump.

The word TAKE is the first bullet point he writes on the blackboard. But Göring presses too hard, and he breaks the chalk. The economic ministers chuckle.

GÖRING

Halt die klappe, you imbeciles!

MINISTERS

Das tut mir leid! Again, sorry, so sorry (*not sorry*).

One of the economic ministers passes a note to his colleague. It has a drawing of a penis penetrating the letter o in the word Göring. The umlauts take on the appearance of tiny, very cold testicles.

Göring presses on. He begins to write a commonly used economics acronym on the blackboard under the word TAKE.

GÖRING

Here's how the program comes together. Okay, I ask you, who owns the majority of properties in Germany?

MINISTERS

Juden!

Göring writes the letter R on the blackboard. It is extra bold. It uses up at least a quarter of the piece of chalk. The word "Juden" is perfunctorily scribbled next to it, like it caused a shooting pain in Göring's wrist as he was writing it.

GÖRING

Correct. So first, we Remove the Jews and their most valuable possessions from their homes. Then we . . .

Göring writes a big bold O next to the letter R.

GÖRING

Then we O*ther* the Juden. Boycott their businesses. Blame them for all kinds of horrendous things—like our defeat in the first World War, poison gas attacks, venereal diseases, degenerate art, gefilte fish.

The Ministers spit on the ground upon hearing the words "gefilte fish," but then one of them whispers, "You know, with a little horseradish, it's not so bad."

MINISTERS

Brilliant, Herr Göring, just brilliant.

GÖRING

Now this next part of the grand economic plan could get tricky, logistically speaking . . .

Göring bears down heavily on the blackboard and writes an extra-thick letter I. Chalk dust is flying everywhere.

GÖRING

The letter I, gentlemen, is for Internment.

The ministers rub their chins thoughtfully and skeptically tilt their heads.

MINISTERS

But we hardly have enough prison space for all of the Juden. Where will we put them?

GÖRING

Excellent question. First, we wall them off in ghettos. While rotting in there, we build new places—camps—where thousands can be crammed together in very small amounts of square footage. And then, we put them to work.

MINISTERS

"Ooh, ooh! How about this for the camp name: WirWorks. Or maybe, WeArbeit."

GÖRING

Nein. Each camp will have its own name; you know how strongly Reich Minister Schacht and I feel about branding.

MINISTERS

I have another I-word for you, Herr Göring—*ingenious*!

GÖRING

Look, I know what you're thinking: we can't intern them forever, it's too costly, and what would happen if they ever . . . returned . . . got out and came back to reclaim what will soon be rightfully ours, setting back the only viable economic stimulus plan we have?

At this point the chalk was just a tiny nub in Göring's hand.

GÖRING

More chalk! Schnell!

A stout minister proffers a new piece of chalk; in his haste, the monocle pops out of his squinting eye. It rolls within inches of Göring's jackboot. He considers stomping on it, smashing it into a hundred pieces. Instead, he picks it up and hands it back to the minister.

GÖRING

You dropped this. Ha, you thought I would crush it under my boot. Don't be a dummkopf. I'm not cruel.

Göring turns his back to the ministers and faces the blackboard. He holds the new piece of chalk aloft, a crossing of swords with Wodan, God of War. He can feel its power vibrating in his hand because what he is about to write on the blackboard will forever change the way war is played.

With exquisite German precision, Göring writes the letter E. The chalk is mightier than the Luger.

GÖRING

E, my dear ministers, is for Extermination. Rest assured, this economic stimulus plan will be a success. The Juden will not be coming home.

Chinese Restaurant

FOSTER CITY, CALIFORNIA

His mouth full of Mongolian beef, my brother speaks.

STEVE

I'm telling you, Dad, your life is a movie. We should pitch it to a studio, see if they'd be interested in making it. Todd, you know people in the business, right?

TODD

I'm in advertising, Steve, the movies I make tend to be in the thirty to sixty second range, often with a strong call to action at the end. I think Dad's story needs a little more time to develop.

STEVE

But wait, there's more! If you act now, we'll throw in a second trauma at no extra cost, you just pay for shipping and handling and therapy . . .

DAD

Fuck a movie about my life. I don't need a movie. A lot of people had it worse than I did.

I also attempt to convince him.

TODD

C'mon, Dad, the way you rode from Germany to Warsaw on top of a fast-moving train? That's cinematic if you ask me. And going through tunnels at high speed meant you could have been decapitated if you chose to enjoy the view at just the wrong time.

DAVE

Oh, so you guys are film producers now? Okay, Hollywood bigshots, who would you get to play me? I see Dustin Hoffman, or better yet, Harrison Ford.

TODD

Uh, sure, Indiana Diamentstein. But I think you're more of a Larry David type, or Alan Arkin, may he rest in peace.

My father thoughtfully strokes his chin, looking off into the auditioning distance.

DAVE

You know something, maybe Mandy Patinkin. Mel Brooks could work . . .

STEVE

Hmmm, I'm seeing Charlie Sheen as Dad. So what about you, Todd, who would you cast to play the genetically traumatized insecure writer?

TODD

Damn, that's a tough question. Um, if it's from the Jew or half-Jew talent pool, I'd have to go with David Duchovny or Ben Stiller, maybe David Schwimmer . . . hmm, Paul Rudd would be cool, Jesse Eisenberg, or, okay, I got it . . . Jason Segel.

STEVE

Did you say Steven Seagal?

TODD

And you? Who should play the part of Steve Diamond?

STEVE

Will Arnet. *Arrested Development.* Brilliant performance in a story about dysfunctional families.

TODD

Well, in that case, get Jason Bateman's agent on the line, he could portray me.

I dramatically bite the head off a large prawn before questioning my father.

TODD

So, Dad, I take it you made it to Warsaw in one piece, head and all?

DAVE

Arrived intact and right on time. But Warsaw? Destroyed. There was nothing there for me. No shelter, no family. You remember when the three of us went there? What was it . . . fifteen-years ago? You guys saw a modern city.

I reflect on Warsaw. The image of bruised remains flood my mind.

TODD

Also a few sections of Ghetto wall that refused to crumble under pressure.

Steve fumbles with his chopsticks, one drops to the floor

STEVE

Pretty remarkable considering Jews were forced to build the Ghetto walls. We're not exactly known for being good with tools.

DAD

There were a couple of agencies on site that tried to help survivors find family. Funny thing . . . I couldn't convince them I was Jewish. My papers labeled me a Christian.

STEVE

Why didn't you just whip out the kosher pickle?

DAD

Steve, what's the matter with you? Okay, maybe I thought about it, but I kept it in the jar because one day, after hours of wandering the smashed streets of Warsaw and finding nothing, I ran into a priest—

STEVE

Oh God, is this going where I think it's going . . . ?

TODD

Oh, okay, now I see us pitching a different movie to DreamWorks: *Diddler on the Roof.*

DAD

Pfff! I ran into a priest who told me to leave Warsaw and go to Lodz. The city wasn't destroyed, and there were several agencies there working to reunite families and help find temporary homes for orphans.

Steve clutches his heart in an over-exaggeration of relief.

STEVE

Oh, thank goodness, praise Jeezus.

TODD

So, Dad, another rooftop train ride?

DAD

No, no, Todd, this time I rode inside the train car.

STEVE

(over-the-top yawn) Booooorrring.

52.6311° N, 22.0531° E

WARSAW (WHAT WAS LEFT OF IT)

MY FATHER RETURNED HOME AND FOUND THIS:

Warsaw was shattered into millions of pieces; I'm estimating 157 pieces for every life lost. The Luftwaffe was fiercely committed to flattening the place, especially after Warsaw resistance fighters dared to rise up. That's when German forces really unloaded. It took a couple of months, but in the end, they destroyed more than 85 percent of the city, providing enough smoke-filled, black-and-white film footage to promote World War II programming on the History Channel for decades.

Arriving in the demolished city broke my father's heart. The train ride to Warsaw nearly broke his body. It must have been like riding a bucking mechanical bull racing forward at fifty mph. Another way to think about it: Have you ever been on an Amtrak train, and you really have to take a piss, and you stand up to walk to the bathroom, and the train rocks you back and forth and bumps you up against seats and bodies along the way, and by the time you make it to the bathroom you've said, "Excuse me, sorry, pardon me," at least a dozen times? Well, multiply that by . . . *a lot*, and you can begin to imagine what it felt like to be outside on the top of a train going from Germany to Warsaw at a pretty good clip.

On a more positive note, Mussolini would have been impressed—the train was on time. You can't always say that about Amtrak.

My father returned home and did *not* find this:

Family. They were pushed into mass graves or, like my grandmother, a single grave, or they were shoved onto cattle cars. Sadly, there was nothing left for him in Warsaw. And how's this for irony . . . he tried, but my father couldn't convince authorities that he was a Jew. His only form of identity pegged him as a Christian, a boy whose last name now ended with the letter i, not a y. He thought about exposing the family jewels but decided it was probably best to keep the nicely "cut" Diamond in his pants.

After a day of searching throughout Warsaw, he finally found a few sympathetic people and compassionate clergy willing to listen to his story. Also, there were several agencies on site working to reunite families and place orphans—whose lives were flattened—into homes that were, remarkably, still standing.

So, another train ride. This time he rode inside the car.

Lodz, Poland

MID-1940s

THE HUNT FOR FAMILY TOOK PLACE AGAINST A BACKDROP OF GRAY SKIES made grimmer and grayer by massive smokestacks pumping coal ash into the air. At least it wasn't the other kind of ash that had rained down on towns within earshot and gunshot of death camps. The low-hanging murkiness of Lodz was pierced by imposing Baroque architecture, most of it completely intact because it was where the German military had set up their headquarters. By the time my father arrived in Lodz, the architects of annihilation had either been arrested, vengefully murdered, were hiding out in South America, or were secretly aiding American rocket scientists in their quest to make a giant leap in the space race. What's more, several former Nazi brainiacs quietly took up residence behind white picket fences in the suburbs of the South—states like Alabama—where they helped guide the design of weapons of atomic mass mayhem. Boy, would I love to hear that severe German dialect blended with a languorous southern drawl: "Heil, y'all."

Lodz was mainly a Christian community, but my father's Jewdar was fully engaged, which meant he immediately sniffed out a Jewish support agency. They were stationed in Lodz to provide vital supplies like soap (free of harmful ingredients such as pure Jewish fat), hand towels, food rations, as well as assist in the reuniting of families after the war. And there, it happened yet again, the whole identity papers and the "Come on, kid, you're not a Jew" nonsense. He was being canceled before cancel culture was ever a thing. He tried to explain his situation, the twisted journey and all the things he lost along the way. He even swore to God (but never on his parents' lives because his father might still be alive). No matter what he did to convince others of his Jewish background, there was simply no room at the Kosher Inn for a boy named Lipski.

Letter i. Letter y. Oh, why bother anymore? It would be so much easier to not break character. The decision was made; he'd cut from Judaism, forsake his membership with the tribes, and unite with the uncut nation. If they thought he was a Christian, well, all right then, he'd be a Christian. So, he split from the Jewish agency, split off from the Jewish religion, and made his way to the Christian Polish Agency. Brace yourselves . . . On the way there, he actually attempted to create a foreskin for a second time, a balls-up fiasco that could have caused permanent damage.

Thanks, Dad, for not stretching and tying up the flesh more than this time or that other time after your arrest in Warsaw while hiding in the bathroom waiting for a physical exam before being shipped off to a German boot factory. Any additional fumbling down there and I might not be pushing letters on this keyboard.

YYYYYYYYYYYYYYYYYYYYYYYYYYYYYYYYYY

Although he was stuck with his cut penis, the rest of his Jewish identity would be left on the cutting room floor back where it all started—in Warsaw. *Lehitraot*, my Jews; goodbye. I'm out. Time to move on, and why wouldn't he? The religion hadn't served him well. Dead parent(s), slave labor, and because he'd been hiding from the Nazis since the age of twelve, no bar mitzvah, although, if you really think about it, the kid had more rites of passage than all of the Hebrew schools in Brooklyn combined.

So, *Presto Corinthianos*! Out with the Old Testament, in with the New. Through a freshly installed filter of Christianity, my father presented an abbreviated version of his young life to a bureaucrat at the Christian Polish agency. The man was deeply moved by the orphan's story and pleaded with him to sit tight because there was a married couple he must meet.

Two hours go by. Three hours go by. My father felt it was hopeless. He would leave, go it alone, renew his search for any surviving family members. But just as he was walking out the door, the couple arrived! I know, cheesy cinematic timing, but that's how it goes for some chosen people who get chosen, even if they've recently made the choice to abandon their religion. (Weighing in as an ad guy, The Chosen People™ is pretty great branding.)

The couple and my father were formally introduced, and the chemistry was right. It was so, so right. The Christian husband and wife made a sweet offer to my father: a place to live and a salary for helping in their stationery store. There would be no cows, no daily beatings or forced confinement, and sadly, no *zaftig Volksdeutsche* for twice daily rolls in the hay. Those antics would occur later, in Israel. But until then, peace, pillows, blankets, and Jesus Christ. Amen.

Although the hasty penile reconstruction was a bust, he quickly learned the ways of the church. Kneel, bow, genuflect, cross himself (that one took a bit of practice), but he figured it out. Such dedication. This was beyond *Actor's Studio* immersion, he made Lee Strasberg method actors look like they were phoning it in. My father became Christian through and through. Then, about two months into his new wonderful goyish life, the couple said they wanted to have a serious conversation with him after dinner. Oh well, it was nice while it lasted. But it turns out, they wanted to take the relationship to the next level; they asked to adopt him. Hallelujah, praise the Lord. The archangel Raphael would watch over my father as he slept that night. This whole being a Christian thing was really paying off.

Alas, it was probably an unconscious decision to throw down the word *lehitraot* on his way out the door of Judaism. (I assume there is a gaudy *mezuzah* attached to that door.) You see, *lehitraot* is indeed how one says "goodbye," however, it also means "see you again."

Chinese Restaurant

FOSTER CITY, CALIFORNIA

I pull my notebook closer and remove
the chopstick bookmark.

TODD

Why didn't you just make it permanent? It sounds like a cushy situation.

My father reaches for his glass of scotch, doesn't pick it up.
Simply places his palm on top, trapping the intoxicating vapors.
The glass and its liquid are on full alert, ready for duty.

DAD

It almost happened, Todd. The couple made all the necessary arrangements to adopt me legally.

TODD

So why didn't they go through with it?

DAD

Why? Why didn't they go through with it? Well, a few days after they talked to me about adoption, I went to Piotrkowska Street. That's the main shopping area. I bought myself a pastry and just kept strolling, looking down at my food, you know, the way you two schmucks constantly look down at your phones.

I discreetly take my phone off the table as my father recounts this part of his story.

DAD

Between bites of pastry, I'd look up, just long enough to catch glimpses of scenery and people passing by. There's an apartment building, a clothing store, a butcher shop, a woman with a dog, an awning in need of repair, my father's brother . . .

I flip through my notebook and land on the pages that concern post-war Lodz and Warsaw.

TODD

Ahh, Uncle Ike. Uncle fucking Ike. That's amazing. What are the odds, but wasn't he—

My father pushes his chair back, stands to go to the bathroom.

DAD

Halt! Stop the interrogation. I need to take a piss. Order me the chicken and asparagus.

Steve reaches down to the front of his pants. In a grand gesture, he lifts his imaginary penis up to his chest and ties it in a big knot.

STEVE

Do you think he's gonna . . . ?

I try not to, but I laugh at the uncut dick joke.

STEVE

Hey, Todd, wasn't Ike a shrewd bastard? I thought he screwed over Dad—something about stealing his visa? Ask him when he gets back.

TODD

I will. But Ike's wife, Aunt Bella, she was so nice, a great cook, and really beautiful.

STEVE

Yeah, Bella looked like Sophia Loren.

TODD

The beauty married a beast.

As Steve and I have our heads down, scrolling through our phones, our father returns from the bathroom. Steve looks up.

STEVE

You finally joined the fraternity of the foreskin?

My father takes a seat, pushes more food onto his plate.

DAD

What the hell are you mumbling about?

I have pen in hand, notebook open, ready to receive whatever comes next.

TODD

Dad, it's really incredible. I mean, the chances of that happening . . . looking up at the exact right moment and there he is, one of your only surviving family members.

STEVE

Not exactly mensch of the month club, though.

DAD

What are you talking about, Steve? Oh, you mean how Ike stole my visa? Or the other, um, sadder . . . uh sure, sure . . . yeah, he intercepted my visa and went to America with it. But in the end, it was meant to be. It forced me onto a different path . . . to Israel. Look, it's complicated. Sure, Ike was a rough guy. But he was my father's brother. You can never understand.

I respond without looking up from my notebook.

TODD

Hmm, I'd tell my kids to punch Uncle Steve in the dick if he stole their visa. Anyway, Dad, can you go back to that first moment when you were reunited with Ike?

My father picks up a small bowl of rice.

DAD

You see this rice? See the color? My uncle went totally white, like he saw a ghost.

STEVE

(nods and smiles)
Like white on rice. I've never heard the expression used so directly.

DAD

Look boys, try to picture it: The street's very crowded, people shopping and strolling, and then I look up, I see a man . . . my God, it's my uncle. Interesting thing was his face. It had barely changed. The war didn't seem to have damaged him as much as everyone else.

TODD

So, what'd you do? You scream out his name?

DAD

I tried, I really tried, but I couldn't speak. So, I just stopped walking, turned around, and jostled my way back through the crowd—

TODD

Like a salmon swimming upstream.

STEVE

A smoked salmon.

DAD

Well, I finally catch up to him and tug hard at his jacket. Oh, he was not pleased about that. But I managed to squeak out a few words. I asked him if his last name was Diamentstein, and then I asked if he was my uncle.

TODD

How insane. What was his reaction? Shock? Did he cry?

STEVE

Did he hit you up for a few zloty?

My father barrels through the harsh interruption.

DAD

Mostly shock. It was like a movie. Ike really lost it; he startled some of the pedestrians.

TODD

I get it. It's incredible. Was Ike with Aunt Bella?

DAD

No, he was alone. I met Bella for the first time right after finding Ike. He took me back to his house for dinner, a really good meal. I remember we had meat and vegetables. Those things were still hard to come by, but Ike was wealthy.

TODD

What'd you guys talk about? How many times did you all go, "Holy crap, I can't believe we're sitting here after all that's happened."

DAD

It was very hard. We shared our stories about surviving; we talked about the family members who didn't make it.

TODD

Is that when you learned about your father?

DAD

Ike shared that earlier. It was the first thing I asked after we found each other.

My father pauses. He's recalling the encounter in his mind. He takes a sip of tea, then quickly switches to his scotch before speaking.

DAD

You guys remember the Umschlagplatz?

TODD

Yep, know it well—the first place we went to on our Poland trip. And where you catch the cattle car for Treblinka.

STEVE

Death Tour '04. Such a fun trip, right Todd? And I got to bring back trauma and nightmares—best souvenirs ever.

I continue writing details down in what seems to be a rare moment of full disclosure.

TODD

Dad, you good? Need a break?

DAD

What I need is more rice, white, not that brown hippie stuff.

TODD

Okay, so, after that, that's when you go to Ike's house?

DAD

That's right. It's also when I first learned the truth about Bella and Ike.

TODD

Truth? What truth?

DAD

Now listen closely sons, you need to know this. Bella was not Ike's wife. She was his mistress.

STEVE

(dramatically imitates iconic sound effect) DUN DUN DUNNNNNNN!

Am I even qualified to do this? Write a Holocaust memoir about my father's experiences? For more than twenty-five years, I've been an advertising copywriter churning out pithy persuasion. I think the most words I've ever strung together was in a brochure for a Microsoft product. So technically speaking, maybe I shouldn't be considered a "real" writer—who do I think I am to even attempt writing the story of one of the Holocaust's last men standing (who now has a little trouble standing). This book-writing is a daunting and intimidating creative process. At best, I know a few hundred words, the capacity of a large box of refrigerator magnet poetry (swear words make up a decent portion of that total), and basically, I just arrange and rearrange those words for my profession and for personal correspondence. And I'm not imagining my deficiencies. Several years ago, a "real" writer who has written important books, including a biography about the life and works of Mark Twain, told me so, right to my face:

Andy was an acquaintance of mine. We were next-door neighbors in Providence, Rhode Island; it's where I landed my first copywriting job (thanks, John Housley).

One evening, Andy was hosting a party at his apartment. His guests included men and women who seemed dressed for a literary fiction costume party. I'd heard about suede patches on tweed sport coats but had never actually seen them up close. I thought it was a fashion fiction, but at this gathering of writers and professors, it was fashion fact, and there was lots of it. At one point, I really had to control the urge to sneak up behind one of the highbrow guests and use my fingernail to deface the animal hides that were providing added protection for sharp, real-writer elbows.

Here's how the insult went down: I was standing in a group, a circular formation with a small gap that I designated as my escape route in case I fell short in the witty banter department. Andy was on the other side, exactly opposite from where I was engaged in a conversation with a woman who taught at Brown University—a professor who'd recently published a collection of short stories. After briefly introducing ourselves, she asked what I did for a living. I replied that I was a writer, and as the words were entering the airspace between us, I caught Andy's eye. He looked at me, or rather, he glared at me, and in a slow-motion gesture of occupational haughtiness, he shook his head and silently mouthed the word, "No." It went on for a few seconds longer than necessary, so it was more like, "Noooooooooo."

Message received. She saw it as well, which consequently resulted in a real-time mid-sentence correction: "I'm a writer . . . um, well, not an actual writer. I'm a copywriter. I write ads."

And then, the "what-the-fuck" freeze-frame moment, like a scene in a commercial when a mother admits to buying a bargain brand of toilet paper for her family's buttholes and the whole store just stops dead in its tracks, aghast at such fecal negligence.

Exposed in a roomful of scholars, I thought about disappearing through the opening in the circle, which at this time had dilated considerably, allowing me an easier escape, but instead of group derision and intellectual harassment, these smarty-sleeves leaned in and wanted to know more about the advertising profession. For example, did I write jingles? I did, for a basketball shoe brand—a rap song—and it would have been an extremely shitty white-dad rap song had a member of Grand Master Flash not been brought on to provide authenticity.

Did I come up with slogans and taglines? Yes, I did. Was it like *Thirtysomething*, the whiny TV series airing at the time? It was, kind of, but with more cocaine and late-night fucking on conference-room tables. All of a sudden, I was "interesting." I was the wacky ad guy, and the people were curious; they wanted to know more. I was Branderati among the Literati. They made me feel like one of them, almost like a real writer.

I was a few minutes into my tales of the ad world when a well-respected author sporting tiny, round eyewear appeared. I had noticed that the majority of guests tended to wear these tiny round tortoiseshell spectacles, unlike ad people and other creative professionals who favor the harsher lines of rectangles to frame their peepers. He walked up to us and then just barreled his way into the conversation to impart an historical reference. Andy was standing next to him.

"So, I hear you're a pretty good copywriter."

"Thanks, yeah. I've won a few advertising awards."

"Well, did you know that F. Scott Fitzgerald was an advertising copywriter?"

"No, that's cool. I had no idea."

"Yeah, he failed at it. Went on to write the great American novel."

Fuck, I stepped right into it.

"Ah, I see. So I agreed with you that I'm a good copywriter, and what you're saying is, historically speaking, good copywriters don't make great authors, Fitzgerald being the poster child for your argument."

Once again, I caught Andy's eye. He looked at me, smiled without showing any teeth, nodded his head and sounded out a self-important, "Mmm hmm."

Unfortunately, the encounter clings to me. I've never been able to shake his accusation. Plus, the guy had serious literary credentials. But then again, isn't that where great editors come in, like Maxwell Perkins? Who knows, without him, Fitzgerald might have been known for the great American bar soap advertisement instead of *The Great Gatsby.*

Huh, maybe in writing my father's story, I should position myself as a narrator—an observer like Nick Carraway?

Man, that's stupid. So very stupid.

DOCTOR'S NOTE

Please excuse Todd's professional insecurities. Low self-esteem, distrust towards fellow human beings, and a pessimistic outlook on the world in general and on the future, may be the dominant message conveyed from Holocaust survivors to their offspring.

Respectfully,
Dr. Yehuda and team

Lodz, After the War

MID-1940s

"DAV . . . DAVID, OH MY GOD. DAVID, YOU'RE . . . YOU'RE ALIVE. I CAN'T believe it," Ike shouted, alarming some of the shoppers. "How long have you been in Lodz? How did you get here? *Gottenyu*, David, *Gottenyu* . . . I have so many questions, David. Come, let's get to a quieter place."

Ike led my father into a café. It was clear the owner knew his uncle. He was warmly welcomed and seated at a table offering the best view of a street that had unwittingly reassembled a busted family. What kind of tips must his uncle leave to receive such fine treatment?

"Two teas, please," Ike said to the waiter. "And pierogi for my nephew."

There was no small talk in this conversation. My father went straight to the toughest question of all: "Was my father sent to a death camp?" he asked his uncle. "Was it Auschwitz, Treblinka, or one of the other camps?"

"Treblinka," Ike answered directly and without hesitation. "Not long after you disappeared. He boarded the train at Umschlagplatz on Stawki."

"Did you ever hear from him? Could he still be alive and looking for us?" my father asked, but in his heart, he already knew the answer.

"If it was Auschwitz, maybe. Treblinka, absolutely not. Only a handful survived, and if my brother was among the few who did get out, he would have found me."

My father took a few small bites of food. A mournful silence lingered between them, refusing to be neutralized. It lasted for a very long time, until my father finally spoke again: "Uncle Ike, how did you survive? Are Aunt Sabina and Lily okay?"

I'm sure you've made dubious decisions in your life, but I'll wager that Ike's dreadful choice eclipses that difficult choice by an old-country mile and a half. Look, there's no easy way to defuse this bombshell, so the best you can do is duck and cover: Ike, it pains me to say, abandoned his wife and child in the Warsaw Ghetto and went into hiding with his mistress, Bella, a woman whose outer and inner beauty lived up to her name.

Ike and Bella waited out the war underground, in a root cellar located on a farm that was fifty miles outside of Warsaw. Ike saw the potential for Jewish erasure early on. He was a shrewd businessman with political connections and the instincts of a survivalist. He knew to hoard gold; it would turn out to be a life-saving currency. His arrangements with a farmer were sealed just days before the Ghetto was sealed off. Bella and Ike slipped out in the middle of the night where they were met by a driver who escorted them to the farm. There, they would live among the beets, turnips, and potatoes until it was safe again to show themselves in the light.

Whenever I reflect on Ike's self-inflicted Sophie's choice, I can't help but picture a split-screen:

> LEFT SIDE: Lily sits on a grimy floor playing with her threadbare stuffed animal. She cautiously navigates Sugar Bear around a small puddle of water. The ceiling has been leaking for weeks. Lily hears a gunshot from the street, it startles her; she instinctively

calls out for her missing father. Sabina rushes over to soothe her young daughter.

RIGHT SIDE: Bella carefully steps around a half-filled basket of turnips. She walks over to a small rectangular table located in the corner of the root cellar. Bella lights a kerosene lamp and hands Ike a deck of French playing cards. They begin a game of *kasztelanskie.*

LEFT SIDE: Lily is hungry. Not much remains of the rations. Sabina breaks off a hunk of bread and tops it with a small dot of butter purchased on the black market. Lily cradles the bread, offers the first bite to her stuffed animal. Sabina smiles, then weeps silently.

RIGHT SIDE: Bella ladles a small portion of stew into two ceramic bowls. Tonight, they are having a savory meal of beet, parsnip, and onion. Ike whispers a prayer of gratitude for the food. He then reaches out for Bella's hand and kisses it softly. She looks into his eyes, smiles tenderly.

LEFT SIDE: Menacing sounds are coming from the building's hallway. There is panicked chatter followed by loud screams. The crash of doors being kicked in. Lily and Sabina retreat to a corner and take cover behind a chair. They hug tightly. One resident, an elderly man, is dragged out of his apartment. He is begging for the punching and kicking to stop. It does stop, but only for a moment. The next sound heard by Sabina and Lily is a body and a suitcase plummeting down a flight of stairs. Lily is trembling; she hugs her mother even tighter.

RIGHT SIDE: There is a forbidding knock on the door to the root cellar. German soldiers? Have they been found? Bella is terrified; she races to Ike's side. Ike grabs a hammer and a small burlap bag filled with gold coins—a bribe. There is a second knock. But this time, the farmer's wife remembered the knocking code: two-three-three-two. Ike pries open the door with one hand, a blunt instrument in the other hand ready to strike. Everything is fine. The farmer's wife had come to deliver a small basket of potatoes and a carafe of fresh milk.

LEFT SIDE: The image is slightly blurred, but I can still see Sabina and Lily's crumbling apartment. They are not there. The place has been ransacked. Furniture is overturned. Cushions sliced open. A bookshelf toppled. The few pieces of dishware they possessed lay shattered on the ground. A verminous piece of fabric, which barely covered the only window in the apartment, has been ripped away. The soldier responsible for the carnage inside the tiny shelter turns to admire his savage handiwork. Before walking out, he points his pistol at Sugar Bear and fires.

RIGHT SIDE: Ike and Bella are curled into one another, arms and legs entangled. Their exhausted bodies are covered in sweat. It is the second time they've made love this day.

Ike brushes a few strands of hair from Bella's face. They drift off to sleep.

Whenever I ask my father what became of the wife and daughter that Ike abandoned, he'll turn his eyes away from me and sullenly say, "Sabina and Lily were never heard from again. That's all you got to know."

Over the years, my father would learn more about the abandonment and tragic circumstances of Sabina and Lily's death. He requested that the details be omitted. However, there is one detail worth noting: When Ike and Bella had their first child together, they named her Lily.

Chinese Restaurant

FOSTER CITY, CALIFORNIA

General Tso (okay, his chicken) and Buddha's Delight meet up at Lazy Susan Circle.

STEVE

Pass the trauma, please.

I cover my eyes with both hands after hearing Steve's comment and wait a few seconds before parting my fingers, creating a v-shaped window to see my father's face. No tears, no rage. I am clear to proceed.

TODD

Did you visit them often in Lodz? Ike and Bella?

DAD

Visit? No, I moved in with them. They *insisted* on taking me into their home. And it's sad, you know, because the Christian couple . . . they were about to adopt me. And I loved living with them. But what choice did I have? I had to go live with my uncle.

STEVE

Sure, why not? The man clearly had an extra kid's bedroom . . .

My father responds scathingly.

DAD

Steve, c'mon, what's the matter with you? Listen, I'll be honest with you guys, I wanted to live with the Christian family, celebrate Easter and Christmas, go to church. They took me in when no one else would. I . . .

He gets very emotional, pauses, fights back tears.

DAD

You wanna know the saddest part? When we said goodbye and she was wiping the tears from my face, you know what she said? She said, 'Tadeusz, we assumed you were Jewish, but it didn't matter. We adore you. Please remember that. Please, always remember us.'

Now my brother is on the verge of tears.

STEVE

Oh come fucking on . . . Okay, okay. A five-minute snark moratorium. But I can't go longer than that. I can't, I just can't.

TODD

This is good, Dad. He's admitting that he has a problem. It's a good first step. Steve, should I set the impulse-control timer?

Steve takes a few deep breaths, warms up like a boxer before stepping into the ring.

STEVE

Nah, I got this. I'll just bite down on a rolled-up napkin when the urge strikes.

TODD

I believe in you, Brother. So, Dad, you ended up living with Ike and Bella. For how long?

DAD

Not long, really, because just as I was settling into my new so-called Jewish life—the sequel—and swapping Easter for Passover—

Steve breaks his contract.

STEVE

Wait, did you really think it through, Dad? Tossing aside the delicious ham-and-raisin sauce for gefilte fish with a dollop of the bitterness of slavery?

DAD

Ah, couldn't find a napkin to chew on, Son?

STEVE

No sir, Daddy Dearest. Moratorium over. I'm back in the snark tank.

My father regroups after Steve's interruption.

DAD

What the hell was I saying? Oh, right. It was a pretty comfortable situation at Ike and Bella's. But it didn't last long. I was a teenager, and when I wasn't working in Ike's hardware store, I'd hang around with other kids, a really rough crowd.

I continue writing in my notebook, capturing facts and details, some of which I'm hearing for the first time.

STEVE

Goyim. I knew it. How many times did Bella have to tell you not to hang around with those *goyim* thugs, huh?

DAD

Not *goyim*, Steve. These hooligans were Jews. Emotionally wounded Jewish kids. A pissed-off confederacy of orphans. Oh, we were all damaged, but there came this point when we stopped vandalizing and breaking stuff because they persuaded us to build something instead—a Jewish homeland, in Israel.

TODD

They?

My father hoists a fist in the air.

DAD

The Jewish Brigade.

Steve mockingly imitates the gesture, puts his fist in the air too.

STEVE

Sounds made up, Dad. They fight alongside the Jehovah's Justice League?

I pull out phone and Google the Jewish Brigade. My father continues to educate us.

DAD

These were tough Jews. Smart bastards too. They were stationed in Lodz, and they knew to recruit us hot-headed orphans. Can you think of a better fighting force to help the Zionist cause?

I start reading a few stats from my phone.

TODD

Says here that the Jewish Brigade was part of the British army, and they facilitated the immigration of Holocaust survivors into Palestine.

DAD

Yeah, right, right. That was their day job, Todd. These guys . . . oh, excuse me, these blokes were self-trained assassins who lived to kill Nazis.

STEVE

C'mon, Dad, you sure this isn't some story you unwashed orphans read in a Captain Marvel comic book?

TODD

(looking at phone)
Nope, all true, Steve. The Brigade formed highly effective assassination squads.

DAD

Tough Jews, I tell you.

STEVE

A bunch of Hairy Dirty Harrys.

TODD

Says here they also smuggled tons of weapons to the Haganah, including small arms and rifles . . .

My father picks up an imaginary rifle, squints his eye, looks through rifle sight.

DAD

PAH . . . PAH . . . PAH

TODD

. . . that one can assume found their way into the hands of certain raging, revenge-seeking, European orphans.

DAD

Seriously, what kid in turmoil wouldn't want to be like these guys? They were offering us a chance to bury a dark chapter and write a different story for ourselves.

TODD

So how do you get to Israel, Dad? Did the Brigade push you through some kind of supernatural Chosen People's Portal?

Lodz, After the War

MID-1940s

BETTER TIMES WERE SLOWLY RETURNING TO EUROPE. IN FACT, POST-WAR Lodz was experiencing a renaissance. New shops and restaurants were opening, the parks provided safe green spaces, and there was certainly no shortage of things for young people to do. So, it's not surprising that, like a lot of teens, my father fell in with a rambunctious group of kids, and not the kind you'd take back to your house for a sleepover. These comrades were combustible, dangerous, an extremely volatile group of juveniles with uncontrollable anger issues. Gentile miscreants? On the contrary, these troublemakers were Jewish—an unwashed pack of orphans and formerly hidden children. They found each other through flyers posted around Lodz, part of a post-war effort to unite the lost youth and gather them up inside meeting rooms tucked deep within dimly lit buildings.

Manic and psychically wounded, the young agitators were desperate to destroy anything in their path. But ultimately, they found themselves wanting to build something instead: a Jewish homeland. An official state of Israel.

The Jewish Brigade organized these nightly gatherings; their main purpose was to recruit for the cause of independence. Orphans were a primary target. After all, young people who managed to survive the war's devastation would make a ballsy talent pool. Many were rabid, several were unhinged. In other words, with a little coaching, they could be molded into spirited freedom fighters.

You need to understand a few things about the Jewish Brigade. First, they were some of the most punishing soldiers in the British Army. What you had there was an undaunted collective of zealous warriors who passionately believed in vengeance, not justice. These seething Hebe warriors were self-trained assassins possessing an incomparable proficiency in the art of whacking Nazis. But they also had day jobs: to facilitate the immigration of Holocaust survivors into Palestine, a job they took very seriously. It is estimated that between 15,000–22,000 Jewish displaced persons found a place in Palestine thanks to the Brigade's rule-bending efforts and their kiss-my-tuchas swagger.

The Brigade's tactical skills didn't stop there. They also smuggled weapons to the Haganah—an assortment of state-building firepower which found its way to the *kibbutz* system and ultimately into the hands of the newly arrived European orphans.

Also worth mentioning is the fact that England didn't become one of the world's leading colonialist empires without a healthy degree of paranoia. In fact, several British officers stationed in Palestine opposed the creation of the Jewish Brigade. They felt a purely Jewish fighting force could pose a danger to their lives. Basically, they were concerned that Jews would rebel against British authority in the region. Aw, come on mates, would a Jew ever bite the hand that feeds it? Of course not. Although, I have heard about a woman who might blow it off with a grenade. Rivka looks fabulous in Israeli army fatigues, by the way . . .

The Jewish Brigade was comprised of mission-driven badasses. The rebel's rebel. They were also terrific team players, uniting with other Holocaust survivors to form crack assassination squads known as the *Nakam*. Loosely translated, *Nakam* means: "We shall hunt down and kill every SS and Wehrmacht officer who dared to toss Jewish bodies into ovens." Their grandest plans featured mass poisonings of the municipal water supply in Nuremberg along with attacks on the prisons detaining

German war criminals. Those plans were thwarted. But at least they dreamed big. How could any post-war Jewish orphan resist a chance to create a new origin story for themselves by joining forces with these Avenger Maccabees? It was impossible to put up a fight against the calling to fight.

These intrepid men and women would soon advance my father and many other battle-ready kids to the only place that would truly welcome them—they would land with a loud reverberating thud on the sacred soil of Palestine.

Chinese Restaurant

FOSTER CITY, CALIFORNIA

My father touches the side of the teapot, checking to see if it still holds enough heat to scald our tongues.

DAD

It all happened rather quickly. I said my goodbyes to Ike and Bella, said 'farewell and fuck you' to harrowing Poland, and headed to Germany where all the harrowing began. And yes, Steve, inside a train, sorry to disappoint.

STEVE

Yawn, yawn, yawn. But why Germany, why not straight to Jewsneyland?

My father thinks for a minute, then refills everyone's teacups.

DAD

Indoctrination. From the train station, we took a bus to Zeilsheim, Germany. Potential recruits slept in barracks. They served us food, gave us new clothes, shared stories about the glory that awaited us in Israel . . .

However, some kids chose to go to America.

TODD

I'm a little confused, I thought this was just like a short layover before heading to Israel.

DAD

Hmm, more like . . . I don't know how to describe it for you two. Um . . . okay, it was like a convention. Different organizations with tents and tables pulling out all the stops to get you interested in joining their cause.

STEVE

Were there booth babes? You know, some sexy Sabra tomatoes?

DAD

Sure, Steve, but also, there was wonderful music and ecstatic dancing—

STEVE

Jeezus, Dad. You went to Zionpalooza!

"Zionpalooza" Zeilsheim, Germany

MID-1940s

BELLA CRIED AS THEY HUGGED GOODBYE. UNCLE IKE? NO WAY. HARDENED bastard. My father and his new wild-eyed friends were going off on a bold and patriotic adventure. Farewell, harrowing Poland, they were leaving you for good.

Destination: back to Judaism's ground zero. But first, they had to make their way back to Germany. They went by train and bus to Zeilsheim, Germany, just outside of Frankfurt where his crew would attend Zionism's version of SXSW—an ideology-fest complete with music, folk dancing, meetings, networking, and *Ted Herzl Talks*: short inspiring lectures featuring a couple of witty opening remarks about diaspora, a sure-fire way to boost your number of "Jiews" (views by Jews).

TED HERZL TALK SPEAKER

"Displacement? Yeah, I displaced my reading glasses. Try reading one of those tiny-print Zionist pamphlets without 'em."

The sass was combined with thought-provoking slides and inspiring platitudes:

- No nation on earth has endured such struggles and sufferings as we have.
- The Maccabees will rise again.
- Restoration of the Jewish State.
- We are a people, one people.
- Oppression and persecution cannot exterminate us.

"And remember, Jews, avoid visual clichés, and never refer directly to your slides, it's nationhood storytelling, not reading."

Barracks were constructed to provide sleeping accommodations for the potential recruits. Healthy food was served, new clothing provided, and propaganda was dished out in huge portions. The young hearts and minds were aggressively infused with strength-and-pride sentiments that were just beginning to reconstitute in European Jews.

The Jewish Brigade and Zionists were out in force. But they weren't the only squad with a God and a purpose who showed up at this conscriptionfest. Mormons, who knew a thing or two about persecution, were on site as well. Sure, their *Ted Herzl Talks* lacked graphic flair and the Yiddish humor deployed by the Zionists, and they couldn't quite grasp how to be self-deprecating, a tried and tested way to lower the cynicism barriers of your audience:

MORMON PRESENTER

"A Mormon walks into a bar . . . but seriously, folks, take my wives, please . . . "

And yet, the Mormons' heartfelt pitch about adoption by American families was powerful and deeply affecting. In fact, several Polish youths destined for the Jewish Holy Land chose a different life in a different Holy Land: Utah.

Understandable. It's tough to compete with the promise of a safe life in America. Plus, I assume the Mormon swag bags included magical undergarments—imagine how much that increased their booth attendance.

But to my father and his friends, any direction other than the Middle East was considered traitorous. By this time, they were fully programmed for farming, fighting, and finding the deepest Jewish roots. The youth were ready for duty and looked forward to the physical demands waiting for them on *kibbutz*, the only way to truly scrub off the grimy nightmares of Europe.

Marseilles, France

MID-1940s

You can't train your way to Israel. You go by boat. To get to the boat, they took a bus to Frankfurt, and after the bus to Frankfurt, they took a train to Marseilles, and from Marseilles, it was approximately two days of not-so-smooth sailing and frequent hurling into buckets before they would reach Haifa aboard the SS *Champollion* (a less murderous, seafaring kind of SS).

There was no room for emotional baggage in the overhead compartments; they'd have to leave it behind. Fine, because now they had only a single carry on: the dream of statehood. And they'd do anything, and cross any line, to ensure it.

"No, God did not go with us on this journey," is how my father responded when I asked if he believed that divine intervention kept him from dying in Europe and having a chance at starting a new life in Palestine.

"God? Judaism? No, not anymore; it only brought misery. Everything was taken from me, from all of the orphans on board. The only thing that kept us going was the Zionist dream, this stirring vision implanted into us before we departed and reinforced throughout the ocean journey.

It was all we talked about. Well, not just that. There were hundreds of us, maybe close to a thousand orphans on that ship. Naturally, we grew closer on that week-long trip, so in between puking your guts out, you'd spill your guts."

"What do you mean?" I asked.

"Like . . . okay, several kids had no idea they were Jews until liberation. They were hidden children, placed into monasteries or cloisters. But they had no love for Jesus, no belief in Christianity, either. We were an existentialist youth group who understood that you can't rely on religion or higher powers to determine your path. Honestly, we felt abandoned by God, by the world. The only things that kept us moving forward were the uplifting patriotic songs and fiery speeches illuminating the Zionist ideology. That was our religion."

"Is it right to say you finally had something to live for?" I asked.

"I think that's right. Look, we were destroyed kids desperately needing a reboot. The opportunity to help create an independent Zionist state, a Jewish homeland born from might, not passive prayers, it was the only thing that could heal us. And I'll tell you, Son, no other feeling in my life—not marrying your mother, not starting a business, not the birth of you or your brother, could match what I felt the moment I saw Haifa come into view."

"C'mon, what about sexy tomatoes, or big titties?" I interrupted.

"Not even that, or those."

How is it that there are still people in the world who ask, "Was it really necessary to establish a Jewish state?" According to the FBI's annual data on hate crimes, Jews are consistently the most targeted religious community in the US.

More breaking Jew News: According to a Pew Research Center survey, half of Americans do not know that 6 million Jews were killed in the Holocaust. From multiple choice answers, 12 percent selected 3 million (they probably think Joe Biden won the popular vote by only 3.5 million), 2 percent selected less than 1 million (if only), another 12 percent said more than 12 million Jews died in the Holocaust (wishful antisemitic thinking), and 29 percent said they were not sure or did not answer (silence is denial).

That's right, only 45 percent of 11,000 Americans surveyed knew the correct figure. To those of you who paid attention in your History of Western Civilization class, congratulations, you advance to the bonus round and a chance to learn that there has been a steady rise in hate crimes against Jews just before and immediately after the Hamas attacks of October 7, 2023, much of it accelerated by social media. In fact, the moment Elon Musk reinstated bigot accounts on X(tremist), the former Twitter, the ADL logged over 5,000 examples of virulent antisemitism. "Shall we ban the ADL from my absolute free speech platform?" asked the titan of many industries. Look, I like you, Elon. You make important stuff; the world needs you. So please do not antagonize the ADL. They have intricate entanglements that can topple influencers who incite malcontents, even those at the apex of the three-comma society.

And one final gem from the ADL: More than 42 percent of Americans either have friends/family who dislike Jews (23.2 percent) or find it socially acceptable for a close family member to support Hamas (27.2 percent).

I SPEAK ON THE PHONE OR ZOOM WITH MY FATHER ABOUT THREE TIMES per week. Typically, each call lasts between fifteen and thirty minutes. However, since October 7, the length of those calls has increased; they are now thirty to forty-five minutes. Which means approximately fifteen minutes per call is devoted to additional discussions about antisemitism, anti-Zionism, and the existential threats against Israel since the recent barbaric assault, which many consider to be the worst one since that earlier worst one in the 1940s, which many consider to be the culmination of a fuckload of other pretty bad ones going all the way back to the first century.

If my math is correct, I've spent around 1,080 minutes listening to my father's unfiltered rage against the rabid antisemitism sweeping the nation and Europe. (Thank God for Unlimited Text, Talk, and Data plans.)

Since I don't have the transcripts, I'll share some soundbites of his thoughts and we'll see if the facts corroborate his emotional take on the matters:

> *"Oh, is that right you fucking putzes, can you even name the river? I know soldiers who patrolled near that river; I made out with a girl in that sea."*

From the river to the sea. It's a galvanizing slogan, it moves a ton of merch, everything from hoodies to prayer candles. Although defenders will say it is nothing more than an aspirational chant, the words are baked into the charter of a terrorist organization. Now, I'm not a political linguist, but if you ask me (and the ADL), calling for a Palestine that completely wipes away more than 7 million of its current occupants is not just anti-Israel, it is wildly anti-Jewish. And while we're on the subject, don't you think it has that unmistakable stench of pro-genocide, as well?

> *"I'm telling you, Son, the antisemitism, it's bad, really bad. Feels like I'm back in Warsaw. You know, they spit at us on our way to the synagogue, I was called a filthy Jew on my walks to school."*

He is correctly feeling the anti-Jew zeitgeist. In fact, here are a few facts, compliments of the ADL: Since the Hamas massacre in Israel on October 7, US antisemitic incidents reached the highest number during any two-month period since tracking began in 1979. Over 2000 antisemitic incidents occurred between October 7 and December 7, many targeting Jewish-owned businesses, synagogues, and college campus Hillels.

> *Speaking of colleges . . . : "You call these places of higher education? Well then, teach some history to these ignorant bastards. There are lessons to be learned from our history, but these schmucks, they don't have a clue about our struggle, what it took to have a rightful homeland after the horrors we've faced for thousands of years. That's our land,* bubbeleh, *and it always has been. Anytime those archaeologists dig around, they find more proof that we were there since the beginning. Sure, okay, you want to protest, go protest, but at least see the entire picture. Israel is now defending itself against the worst attack in generations, and the other side . . . they're the victims? How's that possible, how did we lose the story? Any discussion must start with . . . It all began on October 7th . . . It's as if these privileged assholes, some of them Jewish kids, started watching a TV show in the middle of the series. They not working with the whole plot."*

Well, you don't need a master's degree to know that antisemitic threats, violence, and vandalism are surging across colleges and universities. Many Jewish students no longer feel safe because schools aren't doing enough to protect them. Some pro-Palestinian students (*Team Hamas* as my father categorizes them) are threatening to drop out if their schools refuse to stand against Israel. And several graduations are being cancelled. Which, come to think of it, is probably a good thing. There will be less traffic, hotels won't gouge travelers, and most importantly, please kids, please abandon your elite universities—the world needs more skilled tradespeople.

Chinese Restaurant

FOSTER CITY, CALIFORNIA

My father scrapes the last of the sweet and sour 'in-memoriam' onto our plates.

DAD

Oh, we were screwed up, damaged, a bunch of devastated kids, and there were lots of us, all heading to Haifa on the boat—at least five hundred orphans.

Steve blurts out another "Steve" comment, thinking it might lighten the mood.

STEVE

That's a lot of orphans. You guys consider changing the boat's name to the SS *Oliver Twist*?

My father is turning more somber at this point. He puts his chopsticks to the side of his plate. Seeing this gesture makes us cease shoveling food into our mouths. We immediately realize he's going dark.

DAD

All of our parents were murdered, but at least I knew what happened to mine. Some of the kids, they had zero details, nothing, just that their parents were killed. I thought about my mother constantly, the horrible thing that happened to her, and my father, the way he died in Treblinka . . . gas and oven. I kept thinking that, no matter what comes next, I will never see them again. How can anything feel good after that? If it wasn't for my teacher, Mattityahu, I wouldn't be . . .

He takes a long pause before speaking.

DAD

Listen guys, that wonderful man, he saved me. He brought us back from the dead.

My father remains fixed on his teacup. He twists it clockwise against the white tablecloth as he recalls this bleak moment from his past. Steve and I see heartbreak reveal itself in his tear-filled eyes. The walls of traumatic memory are closing in. And then, BAM!, *he suddenly snaps out of it.*

DAD

Hey, how about we get another order of dumplings. And I better see some cake on this table after dinner. It's my birthday soon.

I am floored by his ability to shake off the horror, how deftly he pivots from the trauma.

TODD

How do you do it, Dad? How do you defy the gravity of despair like that? I've seen it a bunch of times. You go off the emotional cliff, about to crash, but then whoosh, some kind of cognitive jet pack kicks in and propels you back to the surface. It's . . . it's fucking weird.

My father just shrugs.

Steve holds up an imaginary book, licks his index finger, and turns imaginary pages.

STEVE

I believe . . . yes, it's right here in the Modern Holocaust Survivor's Manual. Chapter 8: Denial, Repression, or Suppression. Which Anti-Nazi-Depressant Is Right for You?

TODD

Steve, you remember the train ride to Krakow?

Steve starts shadow boxing.

STEVE

Of course. Part of Death Tour '04. The side trip to Auschwitz to give Dad a chance to stretch his misery muscles and let him spar with that mass murder before climbing into the ring at Treblinka.

TODD

Right. Those personal demons are like doped-up MMA fighters.

My father tries to stay out of the banter, but he knows where it's heading, so he volunteers the intro to the story.

DAD

This again, Todd? My little outburst when we passed by Ike and Bella's beet bunker?

TODD

Yep. I had headphones on, so I couldn't really hear it at first, but you were staring out the train window and sobbing uncontrollably. You just about started wailing.

I look at Steve and make the motion of a film set clapperboard. It's obvious we've done this routine many times while growing up.

Steve kicks it off:

STEVE

Roll sound . . . and ACTION!

I seamlessly pick up Steve's direction and melodramatically act out our father's distress–with a bad Polish accent.

TODD

. . . My God, *Gotenyu*, Oy, my God, I think this is where my uncle was hiding with Bella. The farm, the root cellar—potatoes and turnips and beets OHHHHH MY . . . The farm, it's here.

STEVE

CUT! Great take, Todd. Exactly how I remember it. Let's move on.

TODD

And then you did that shock-pivoting thing, where, in just a split second, you erect an emotional dam, completely cutting off the river of tears, and you simply ask . . .

I once again imitate our father—my Polish accent is getting worse, if that's even possible.

TODD

. . . So, either of you putzes up for a game of rummy?

STEVE

Cut! Think we've got it.

Without warning, my father detonates, slams his palm onto the table. Liquid erupts from teacups and spills over onto the tablecloth.

DAD

NO, YOU CUT! YOU KNOW-NOTHING CALLOUS IMBECILES. THAT'S ENOUGH! I'VE HAD IT WITH YOU TWO. That wonderful woman, my sweet aunt Sabina . . . left alone to die in Warsaw. Murdered. And my innocent cousin Lily, just a kid. How God, how could you let her be killed by those psychopaths? A child? And you two morons make your little jokes, trying to be so fucking clever.

A few of the other diners are rightfully startled. The owner of the restaurant begins to walk over, to see if everything is okay. I nod reassuringly, wave her away.

STEVE

Dad, we're just—

My father pushes back from the table, angrily throws his napkin. It misses the chair, hits the ground. He storms out of the restaurant.

STEVE

Wow, he really had a problem with your acting.

TODD

Must've been the shitty accent. I've really got to work on that. Should I go after him?

STEVE

Give it a few minutes. We might have stepped on the third rail of Treblinka's train tracks. It's fine, he usually makes a quick comeback. Resilience, a survivor superpower. What about you—what's your recovery time from a rough memory, or when your kids infuriate you?

TODD

Hmm, no more than five or six minutes, plus seven days. Dad, he snaps back, a fancy phrenic skill he developed for survival: Sad/not sad. Angry/not angry. And me, the youngest Holocaust offspring? I just snap, then straight to boil before the long marination in rage and exhausting disappointment takes hold. The misery sets up camp in my brain and pours even more acid into my gut. And because misery loves company, it invites self-doubt, gloom, and joylessness to join in on the anguish party. I just have to ride it out, Steve. But the fucking relentless reverberation of the thing that pissed me off, the anger and the melancholy, it lingers. I can't just unload my fury the way Dad does.

STEVE

Did you mean to say my fury or Mein Fuhrer?

TODD

Don't, Steve. Seriously. It's a fucked collection of behaviors. Caused a lot of collateral damage. Too many personal and business relationships have been smothered by my shutting out and shutting down. Meditation, medication . . . you can't de-energize the mental hellhounds; they depart when they want to depart. Usually long after I need it to happen. You've seen it full blown in all its *gory*—the marriage collapse, the business tanking. You helped me through that shit. But really, Steve, any kind of intense provocation or deep loss and I'm in the dissociative ravine for way too long, dragging down people I care about. My kids definitely know the signals. They know to stay at a safe distance physically, and up to this point, genetically.

Steve reaches for his half-empty glass of scotch. Downs it. I take a few deep breaths to push away the approaching panic.

TODD

And what if we lost him, Steve? He's ninety for fuck's sake. He wants his story told, but what if he checks out before it gets out there? How will I manage through that epic fail?

Steve reaches for our father's unfinished glass of scotch. Downs that as well.

STEVE

Well, I imagine that each time you look up to heaven to converse with our deceased father, clouds will gather in the sky to form the word PUTZ.

Steve mockingly throws his napkin to the ground, a nod to our father's blowup.

Motherfucking son of a bitch, fuck me, why do you get to inherit all the cool survivor vibes from our father. It's not fair.

TODD

Just luck of the genetic dice, I guess. Speaking of . . . you do know that the Third Reich twisted your second-generation genes as well?

STEVE

Right, my minor "avoidance" addiction: hooked on poker.

TODD

And video poker. And blackjack. And craps. And roulette. And sports betting. And watching sports. And Lotto tickets. And . . . am I missing any escapist games of chance?

STEVE

That about covers it. But really, bro, I'm surprised you could remember all of that. Especially since in some of the medical journals I've read, excessive and prolonged use of cocaine, quaaludes, poppers, MDMA, ketamine, Ambien, psilocybin, anti-depressant-of-the-month, and Mountain Fucking Dew can mess with your memory, Todd.

TODD

Fuck, I had a witty retort . . . what was it?

Before we ventured too much further into the recitation of inherited trauma symptoms, my father appears at our table. He seems calm and . . . what the hell? . . . He has a smile on his barely wrinkled, nonagenarian face. How's that possible? After all the guy's been through, he managed to fend off many of the visible signs of aging. As anyone can see, the frown lines and deeply-set "triangle of sadness" creases did not circumvent the faces of his collagen-depleted sons.

DAVE

One of you schmucks drink my scotch? Actually, I could use some hot tea, where's that waiter?

TODD

Uh, hey Dad, are you good? You need a break?

DAVE

A break? Why would I need a break. Tea is what I need.

Steve leans across the table, puts his hand on my father's arm.

STEVE

You seem pretty calm, Dad, kind of at peace. Did you meet up with the Dalai Trauma on your little walk?

TODD

My Buddhapun bruddah! You nailed it hard, and you don't even know it. The Dalai Lama says, "A true hero is one who conquers his own anger and hatred." Or something along those lines.

STEVE

Well, then, you are one of the least heroic fellows the post-world-war world has ever known.

I raise my two middle fingers, place them together, and bow serenely.

TODD

Allow me to share my two-word mantra . . .
So, Dad, if you're up for it, how about we do Israel as a final main course and then Treblinka for dessert?

DAD

I can go as long as you want. And order as much as you want, 'cuz you're paying.

TODD

Yeah, I think you've paid enough.

DOCTOR'S NOTE

Please excuse Todd and Steve's heightened vulnerabilities to stressful events. Our studies concluded that Holocaust Survivor Offspring (HSO) families were characterized by more intense conflicts within families, unpredictable emotional reaction, and less family cohesion. Furthermore, there is an increased occurrence of mood disorders, anxiety disorders, and substance abuse in HSOs.

—Kindest regards,
The Icahn School of Medicine

Haifa, Palestine

MID-1940s

ACCORDING TO *BLOOMBERG NEWS*, THIS IS HOW KIBBUTZ RAMAT Yohanan is classified today:

Sector: Industrials

Industry: Manufactured Goods

Sub-Industry: Rubber and Plastic

When my father arrived at Ramat Yohanan in 1946, it was less industrial and more agricultural, which was perfect since he had aced his cow-milking training at the Schlochau Slave Academy. His hard-earned farming scholarship quickly vaulted him to Chief of Teats at Ramat Yohanan, responsible for making sure his crew of lactose baristas were correctly pulling shots for the morning *kibbutznik* rush.

Holy cow . . . wait a sec, is that the reason my father is obsessed with large breasts? Too easy. That is so Pop Psych 101. There must be a more complex reason, more oedipal. Perhaps it is due to his early traumatic maternal loss which triggered an ongoing quest for ample bosoms of comfort? Nah, probably just tugging on udders all those years.

The young teenage arrivals from Europe were anything but bright-eyed and youthful; they were old and dispirited souls who had seen too much at an early age. It's nice to believe that the fresh sea breezes between France and Haifa would have revived them, but unfortunately, it just made them hang their heads over the ship's railing, chumming the waters with the last remaining bits of the horrors stowed away in their psyches.

It's no easy feat to extract details about Israel from my father, especially the darker soldiering parts. He did, however, admit that as the War of Independence raged on, orphan rage would be rewrought and ultimately put to lethal use at the appropriate times. (If you're wondering what "lethal" means, so am I; he ain't sharing that level of detail. And trust me, I've tried.) Until then, before the orphan heat was unleashed onto the desert landscape, deep into Arab villages and behind British defenses, the rescued children needed to grasp what it meant to be part of a collective. This was not easy for my father or for any of the child survivors, and they put up a formidable resistance. In fact, the surge of emotionally scarred youth proved to be a profoundly challenging problem for the early pioneers and leaders at the *kibbutz*. Still, they hypothesized that youthful raw emotions could quickly be converted into a powerful force of statehood energy. Unfortunately, these kids were not only damaged, they were also wild. *Wild.*

And as my father pridefully pointed out, "Only one man in the entire Middle East could tame us."

Music soothes the savage orphan. That, and a lot of guidance and mentoring. The teacher who would break these wild ponies was Mattityahu Shelem. An iconic songwriter, Mattityahu was born in Poland and immigrated to Palestine in 1922. After years of early pioneering, he packed up his instruments and moved to Kibbutz Ramat Yohanan in 1941. There he worked as a shepherd, "drawing artistic inspiration from the meditative shifts he put in with the flock."

DJ Mattityahu dropped some dope *bleats* and soon became famous for his Zionist folksongs. I can't say if he was the Dylan of the Desert, or Jew Tang Clan, but here's a taste of his talent:

> "Simhu Na"
> Let us celebrate and throw off our burden! It's a joyous holiday for us; a great day for us.
> We have created something out of nothing
> With the hand that sows and plows.
> Flint rocks and stones flow with abundant waters;
> Strength, might, and courage.
>
> Awake, awaken and be revived among the sickle bearers!
> Persist in work and toil;
> The strength of our spirit should not fall, Awaken, awake.

Can you picture it? Strong, suntanned bodies sitting around a campfire under biblical skies, a shaggy-haired guitarist strumming uplifting ballads about nation-building and working the land. We're talking rousing indoctrination carried upon a few simple chord progressions. And it worked. Even "The Crazy 6" fell into line.

Who were the Crazies? It was Shlomo, Henry, Shimon, Asher, my father, and that terror in a tight sweater, Rivka.

That's what they were called by the other *kibbutzniks*. Four men shy of a Crazy *minyan*, The Crazy 6 wore their badges of hellraising with tremendous pride. That is, until Mattityahu intervened—not to extinguish their violent tendencies, just to tone it down, calibrate the zeal. After all, you didn't dare sand away the sharpest orphan edges; they'd be needed when the real fighting and action broke out.

Mattityahu was a wise headmaster. He was also a father figure and, most importantly, a bottomless pit for orphan despair. He could take the darkest pages of their life stories, scratch out the words Europe, Death, and Loss, and in their place write Rejuvenation, Statehood, and Persistence—words of empowerment, not victimhood. He would carry away their painful remembrances and exchange them for hard labor that yielded nourishment for body and soul.

During his years at Ramat Yohanan, Mattityahu played a vital role in my father's healing. As my father puts it, "He made me a human again—whole."

Mattityahu also prevented my father from recklessly taking his own life.

Of the Crazy 6, it was Shlomo who advanced to the position of Best Friend and Brother. He and my father did everything that two wild and crazy *kibbutzniks* could do together.

Nothing too contemptible. Their antics were family-friendly, rated ג *(gimel)*. Because really, there wasn't much free time for unfettered misdemeanors under such a strict schedule of work duties, which included serving meals, milking cows, tending to the chickens, facilities maintenance, laundry, school lessons, metalwork, preparing the orchards, plus learning to lob grenades, put a bullet in your enemy from a distance, slice open a throat, and burn buildings to the ground.

You see, Mattityahu wasn't the only educator at Ramat Yohanan; there were guest lecturers as well . . . from the Haganah.

Compared to the more extreme activities of the Irgun, Palmach, and Stern Gang, Haganah operations were on the moderate end of the Defense of Statehood spectrum. Until they weren't. The British presence, and their refusal to open up Palestine to unlimited Jewish immigration, left the Haganah no choice but to intensify their tactics.

There came a point when just hearing the imperious British accent would transform a self-restrained Bruce Banner-type *kibbutznik* into a Haganah Hulk, bursting with rage and bomb-making skills that targeted bridges, rail lines, and the despised ships used to deport unwanted Jewish immigrants. Those Crazy 6 quickly became crazy good underground fighters.

I asked my father if I could interview the surviving members of the Crazy 6. Strictly fact gathering, not *ProPublica*-level investigative journalism. Really, I just wanted to get a better understanding of this part of my father's story and attain a clearer picture of what makes him *him* and maybe get some insights into the events that caused his sudden departure from Israel—like why he abandoned the state that he fought to create for a new, uncertain life in America. When pressed on the issue, he always offers up some banal bullshit reasoning, or he'll attempt to throw me off the putrid scent of scorched sands and state-building brutality by telling me he had family in America and that he was on a mission to "bang a bunch of Brooklyn broads." Perhaps there is some truth to that rationale. He did, after all, end up marrying a woman from East Flatbush.

Permission to probe denied. Even if I had been granted access, two of the Crazy 6 have passed away. Two suffer from Alzheimer's. And one harshly stated to my father that he would never, ever talk about what happened in Israel with a "pampered *schmendrick*" like me.

Chinese Restaurant

FOSTER CITY, CALIFORNIA

A WAR BREAKS OUT IN THE MIDDLE OF EVERY MIDDLE EAST DISCUSSION we have. You could bring in leaders from The Center for Conflict Resolution and Seeds of Peace to moderate. And still, no peace. Engage Jimmy Carter, Bill Clinton, and Madeline Albright to referee the talks (in her prime, Ms. Albright could leg press 400 pounds—you don't want to piss her off). No help, there'd still be tension.

Even if the ghosts of Menachem Begin, Shimon Peres, Anwar Sadat, and Yitzhak Rabin were summoned by seance, you would not have conversational peace.

But I'm trying to write something here and to think like a journalist, so I go for it, and ask why they carried out so many assaults against the British. Weren't they mediating, trying to keep the peace between Jews and Arabs?

Wow, the look he gave me . . . the "where-did-I-go-wrong-as-a-father" look, like, how did I not understand the political situation in the Middle East at that historical time. Didn't they teach me anything at college?

Hebrew heat rays emanate from his affronted eyes and singe my beard. He speaks angrily.

DAD

Cocksuckers. The British were the worst bastards in the *Middle East*—they just carved it up, and while they were at it, they created Jordan, and then we had to deal with them too.

He takes a breath, downs the remaining tepid tea, slams the cup onto the table.

TODD

When you say, "deal with them" . . . can you expand on that?

DAD

What do you think? You've asked me questions about my time in Israel for thirty years, and for thirty years have I ever told you anything about the military stuff?

He never has; he never will. Not with any real details, at least. But I thought since he was all hopped up on oolong, soy sauce, and scotch, he might slip and divulge additional details about his more covert activities—the shit that he and the other five Crazies got into.

DAD (CONT'D)

Putz, I don't know what you're talking about. There's

> nothing to tell. Oh, maybe we stole a few eggs or got into a couple of fights, but it was innocent. We milked cows, studied . . . we were kids.

Thing is, my father did cough up some jarring information regarding his participation in guerrilla maneuvers against Arab and British forces. The partial disclosures occurred during our emotional visit to the cemetery at Ramat Yohanan, standing at the foot of the grave of his dearest friend, Shlomo.

Kibbutz Ramat Yohanan

LATE 1940s

Golden Gate Park

LATE 2001

I IMAGINE MOST MIDDLE-AGED MEN WHO GO FOR A STROLL IN THE PARK with their father on an autumn day will discuss things such as the sudden brilliance of the leaves, or perhaps they'll gush over a grandchild's report card. They might chat about the performance of their respective retirement accounts, or whether Icy Hot does a better job on the joints than BENGAY® Ultra Strength. However, on this particular day at the beginning of a new century—and I don't know whether it was the extra espresso shot in his latte or post 9/11 vibes in the air—but when I jokingly said to my father in a childish voice, *Daddy, please tell me a Zionist wartime story before beddy-bye,* he gruffly responded, *Okay putz, you want a story, I'll give you a story.* To which I responded, *Dad, it's fine, I know you hate talking about that shit.* And then he shot back, *Putzface, do you want a story or not?* Which was followed by my brilliantly thoughtful reply, *Uh, sure . . . really?*

So . . . we're at Kibbutz Ramat Yohanan. Most of our weapons were hidden in an area near the back of the cow sheds, buried underground in wooden caskets, deep enough in the earth to avoid being discovered by

British soldiers and their metal detectors. But because of escalating confrontations with Arab fighters from nearby villages, those weapons of mass independence were being brought to the surface with greater frequency.

On a day in 1947, I'm pretty sure it was Shabbat, our *kibbutz* came under fire; it was an ambush. Shlomo and I were quickly dispatched to a hilltop where we'd have a better vantage point to fight back against the assault. We kept our heads down, pressed our bellies to the earth, and held our calloused fingers against rifle triggers that were just itching to be squeezed. But we were damn good soldiers, disciplined, and dutifully deployed our rigorous training—maintaining composure while under a fierce attack.

You getting this, Son?

Now understand, the situation was hot. Sniper shots were flying from two directions. Our *kibbutz* commander ordered us all to stay low and hold our positions. But then, out of the biblical blue, bullets exploded the dirt just inches in front of us. A line had now been crossed. Seeing holy soil fractured by enemy gunfire, well that just activated the deepest rage that lived inside—one of the few things that came with us on the long journey from Europe.

Fuck it! Enough! It was time for reprisal. I sprang up from my defensive position, determined to take out the bastards that would dare pierce the land of our Zionist dreams. Shlomo rose, too, exploding off the starting blocks, charging ahead like a sprinter with a doping habit. Without any warning, he charged at me, tackled me, and shoved my body back to the ground. To make sure I stayed there, Shlomo knocked the wind out of me with a swift boot kick to the stomach. And then, he raced forward on his own, screaming, "For Israel! For Israel!" while unloading his rifle with every stride.

Um, give me a sec . . .

Okay, I'm good, right . . . so . . . within seconds, my dearest friend in the world was cut down by a sniper's bullet. Immediately after the shot brought down Shlomo, several other *kibbutz* soldiers picked off the snipers; they were just a few seconds too late.

Shlomo collapsed a few yards from the hill. Beautiful, brave Shlomo; an emerging country warrior from the old country was slain, a friend who sacrificed his own life to save mine.

It would take several days to regain my voice. I screamed and cursed at God for hours and hours because, yet again, another innocent life in my hard fucking life had been taken away too soon. But my vocal cords weren't the only things shredded in the aftermath. To cope with the loss, I summoned an inner fury and pounded on a *kibbutz* wall with bare fists until the wall cracked and the back of my hands were covered in blood. That's right, God's plaster proxy crumbled from the beating. But there was no cornerman to stitch things up. So I just wrapped my hands in an already bloodied T-shirt.

I had to go on, Todd. But how? Orphan. Soldier. My intense anger, it couldn't be contained, not after seeing my friend die right next to me. Only revenge could heal the loss, even if it killed me.

Don't give me that look . . .

Yes, of course I was prepared to die. A Jewish State; nothing else mattered. We had to survive, the cause had to survive, even if it meant this is where my contribution might come to an end.

Mattityahu, though, he wasn't about to let that happen. My teacher, my mentor, he swooped in to save me from any self-destructive acts of vengeance. You see, Son, the whole revenge business is taken to an entirely different level in the Middle Eastern countries. Literally biblical proportions. And so, like all those who pledge allegiance to eye-for-an-eye justice, I could never allow Shlomo's death to go unanswered; five eyes for that eye. And then some. Normally, it takes a village to raze a village, but in this case, a secret solo mission was planned to avenge the loss of my truest friend: My *mishpocha*, my *bruda* Shlomo.

Retribution, I was obsessed with retribution. Sleeping dogs would not lie. Cheek would not be turned. Bygones would not be bygones. Only a disproportionate response shakes your fucking enemies, or that's how a certain line of Israeli thinking goes. Also, I had a unique power:

Zero-Empathy. That's because the Zionists planned ahead; they embedded an empathy kill switch into us orphans. Motherless, fatherless, we were fueled by visions of a Motherland. Victimhood would be transformed into statehood—by any means necessary.

Ceasefires? De-escalation? You fucking kidding me?

Over several days, I gathered up the necessary materials to shred a sufficient amount of bodies responsible for the assault along with a couple of gas cans containing enough guerrilla juice to smoke several buildings that housed those killers. And it's not like I had a *Rambo: First Blood* poster hanging in my locker for reference; this was all original thinking. But, before I could execute my suicide mission, Mattityahu caught wind of the vengeful plan. And just before heading off on *Operation Shlomo's Revenge*, he tracked me down. I remember our eyes locking; he had such a penetrating stare. Mattityahu took my face into his warm hands, kissed the top of my head, and, in a measured voice that was partly rabbinical and partly Mafia boss, he tranquilized the situation in a single sentence: "Relax, David. Mourn the loss of your friend. *We will take care of it*," he assured me.

They sure did, Todd. And that part of the story, well, you won't ever get that out of me. Never. Nighty night, baby boy.

Electchester Apartments, Queens

MID-1970s

THE ISRAELI ARMY INVADED OUR APARTMENT.

Day after day, I had their intractable sensibilities drilled into my head. For example: "If someone hits you with a stone, you hit him with a Sherman tank, and then you obliterate their home and humiliate and destroy several generations of the sonofabitch's family while you're at it."

An eye-for-an-eye was merely a vengeance appetizer for our people. Active retaliation and a willingness to extricate and displace anything that stood in the path of nation-building (or pancake-making, as you'll soon see), were some of the values passed onto me by my father. Which is why—and I cannot stress this enough—children who come from that kind of background should be watched extra closely.

Especially in seventh grade home economics class.

Someone, anyone, please tell me what the New York City Board of Education was inhaling when they came up with that idea. Give young boys access to any device that can broil, bake, boil, or sear, and you are asking for combustion. Why not offer blacksmithing as well? It's incredible to think that teachers allowed us to be in the same room with items that could reach a temperature of 500 degrees Fahrenheit. And yet, there we were, dull minds surrounded by sharp, heat-conducting objects.

When appliances with the potential to inflict pain are within the reach of seventh grade boys, you will likely witness a rapid escalation of violence. Now imagine if a dangerous device found its way into the hands of a boy who was raised on the controversial book of Exodus rules. Well, prepare for a literal Hell to break loose.

There was another kid in this cooking class—a friend of mine—but he was unlike the rest of us earthlings: Steve Handelman. He had a gift. His hands had been kissed by Apollo. Boy, could he play guitar. He played guitar the way " . . . Ziggy played. He took it all too far, but boy could he play guitar."

Why, Steve? Why did you have to take it all too far?

"Hands." That's what we called him (an obvious nickname). He had been showered with the very same stardust that fell upon Ziggy. This guitar virtuoso was quite a thing to see, especially through clouds of smoke. Here is what I saw through those weed clouds: Steve's frantic left hand flying across the neck of a Les Paul, groping it, strangling it. I saw a pick wildly attacking the instrument, pushing tension to the absolute limit, to that fuck-yeah rock and roll moment just before strings break free.

Here is what I heard through those clouds: raw renditions of "Purple Haze," "Gimme Shelter," and "Brown Sugar" bouncing off the walls of his basement-level bedroom.

If Janis Joplin was ovulating and she found herself in a freaky foursome with Jimmy Page, Keith Richards, and Marc Bolan, Steve Handelman would appear approximately seven months after this rocking orgy. (I'm predicting a premature delivery due to the high probability of illicit substance intake during Ms. Joplin's pregnancy.)

Those hands, man, they were something to see. And something to fuck up.

Why, Steve? Why did you have to take it all too far?

So, what could possibly happen if you give a young guitarist a regular old dishtowel, and then you give another kid—the progeny of a father who survived genocidal killers in Europe and subsequently trained with Zionist warriors of the Middle East—a metal spatula, the kind commonly used to flip pancakes? I'll tell you what happens: hurt happens. Very. Serious. Hurt.

Anyone out there know what a rat tail is? It's when you take a cloth item, a dishtowel, for example, and you soak one of its corners. Then you twist up the towel the way a cowboy would twirl a lasso, making it nice and tight. Now imagine that this particular action is taking place in the fluid and talented hands of Steve Handelman. And now, think of me, son of the *Creature from the Black Irgun* with his back to Steve, diligently watching tiny little bubbles form in a carefully prepared batter as it heats up in a cast iron skillet. I was probably humming a Bowie tune, just minding my own pancakes.

Well, here's what happens next. Handelman, brandishing a wet towel newly transformed into a rat tail, pulls back the cloth and promptly releases it: CRACK!

A dishtowel becomes a propulsive weapon that rips through the flesh of my neck. The sting is agonizing. But I absorb it, suppress the tears. I suffer in silence.

But inside, inherited Holocaust-orphan level rage is building, and the voice of my father dances inside of my head. It has a slight Polish accent, but I understand enough. I know what action must follow. I do not turn around; no way will I acknowledge the ambush. Instead, I simply tend to my exquisite breakfast creation.

Handelman goes back to his business. I take the skillet off the burner, but I do not turn it off. I plate the pancake. A generous amount of powdered sugar is sprinkled on top.

Next, I take the metal spatula used to liberate the finished pancake and place it on the burner. The spatula quickly heats up. I casually glance around the room and see that everyone is engaged in their respective cooking projects, including Handelman. Good. This red-hot kid and his red-hot spatula are now ready for duty. Handelman is standing at a kitchen sink, his left hand resting on a tile countertop. The target is now in plain sight. Let the retribution begin . . .

The flesh of a hand being scalded by a searing metal utensil is neither pleasant to see nor nice to smell. In case you were wondering, when something that hot contacts human skin, it does not lift up easily. It wants to adhere and enjoy the ride a little longer. Eventually, it does come off, right about the time when the victim's initial shock concludes and his merited wailing begins.

The only thing to rise above the chaos and blaring distress of the guitar virtuoso was the teacher's fiery castigation of the entire class, which was far louder and shriller than any smoke alarm.

Although I was the lone perp, the Disaster Master Chef who whipped up a sizzling handful of Haganah-chos, nearly everyone in the room, except for Cynthia, the future valedictorian, and Audrey, the future salutatorian, was deemed to be complicit. However, once the smoke of the incident cleared, only two loyal friends—Jews, by the way—confessed to witnessing the aftermath of the crime, but they couldn't "recall" who'd committed it. The tribe stuck together. They refused to rat me out, and consequently joined me in detention for two weeks.

The upside? We missed two weeks of Hebrew school.

The really serious fucking downside? The call from the teacher to my home. And wouldn't you know it, my father, a man who never answers a phone during dinner, saw the smallest hint of uneasiness in my face as the phone was clamoring for attention. Damn that Israel Defense Force sixth sense; it misses nothing. My father got up from the table, grabbed the phone's receiver, and walked around the corner, stretching the tightly-curled cord until it completely straightened. The conversation lasted too many minutes, which meant my father's food was getting cold, which meant even more punishment on top of the punishment that was about to drop onto my world.

"Uh huh. I see. Well, I'm terribly disappointed. I'll be sure to reach out to Steven's parents. Thanks for calling. I can assure you, we'll take care of it."

Burning flesh. Ovens. Screaming. Chaos. You'd think it would cause my father to experience a series of flashbacks to the camps or to his incendiary zealotry in Israel.

Not exactly.

Every second he was on that call, all I could think about was the potential David Hurt Variations: a belt lashing across my ass, three months grounded, no allowance for . . . forever, military school . . .

Not quite.

The fact is, the conversation provoked a profound moment of self-examination for my father. He understood that on some level, my overly aggressive, perhaps disproportional response was enabled by an unfortunate but necessary philosophy deeply rooted in Jewish survival—transformative teachings that he instilled in his children at impressionable ages: the nurture vs. nature part of our inheritance.

Now, you might find this inconceivable, but my father did not administer a disciplinary measure or steep justice for the iniquity against my pal's appendage. Instead, my father reached out, swaddled my hands with his hands and placed a gentle kiss upon the patriarchal encasement. All he said was, "I'm sorry this happened, Son. Tomorrow we will go to Steven's house, and *we* will apologize."

So, did my retaliative invasion cause Steve's guitar career to go down in flames? Well, the attacker (I prefer freedom fighter) would constantly fret over whether his hand would ever glide across the frets again. I'm pleased to report that yes, his hand did dash up and down the neck of the guitar, just as it always did. But since the victim was a true artist without even the slightest trace of eye-for-an-eyeness, he quickly forgave me and converted his receding wound into more incredible riffs that would've made Jimmy Page go, "Yeah, that's fucking all right, man."

And so, for a few more rocking years after the burning, our friends would take their usual front-row seats on the sofa in Handleman's basement, watching and listening to the boy and his guitar. Nothing could keep our Ziggy and the stardust apart.

Looking back on it, a note of appreciation goes out to the New York City Board of Education for their wisdom and foresight. Turns out, it was a very good thing that the incident occurred in home economics and not in blacksmithing class, where a vindictive kid raised with some of the more extreme Israeli moral codes, might have had a hammer instead of a spatula in his very vengeful hand.

Want to see those hands in action and see that he's still rocking so fucking hard after all these years?

https://www.youtube.com/watch?v=n7FAtyj8Th4&t=152s

Shlomo's Grave, Ramat Yohanan

2004

HAGANAH TRAINED. IRGUN ADJACENT. ON THE MYERS-BRIGGS PERSONality test, my father would chart out as an ISTJ ח׳. Which means he is introverted, keeps to himself, and attains success through dependability. People with this personality type are observant, carefully think through plans, and will determine what actions to take based on logic . . . unless, of course, a friend's body is torn apart by a sniper, in which case, fuck logic; he runs straight toward the danger and somehow remains alive. Hence, the ח׳.

That's what I concluded after listening to my father finally disclose some potent details about what he'd done for the sake of Israel and to honor his fallen friend, Shlomo—the young man who saved his life, the teenage corpse whose bones now lay beneath the ground before us on our visit to Ramat Yohanan.

Although he has consistently stated, "Ask me a thousand times about my years in Israel, and I will never give you an answer," being in the presence of Shlomo's grave produced some plucky tales of war. Which, unfortunately, I cannot share. I promised. Trust me, you do not want to feel the wrath of a war orphan/Zionist zealot.

Therefore, in the interest of state secrets and my own personal safety, the following graveside narratives have been tightly redacted. You'd have to be part of an elite intelligence-gathering bureau (wink, wink) to figure it out.

For example, what happened after Shlomo was gunned down by sniper fire? I'll never tell . . .

Shlomo
village burn

We also learned about a few notorious Rivka incidents. She was by far the most punitive of the Crazy 6. But you didn't hear it from me . . .

Rivka flirt
British officers in Jeep
grenade
BOOM!
BOOM!

There was always a hint of sexual tension in the stories about Rivka. However, my father swears that there was nothing romantic between him and the freedom fighter . . .

my father
Rivka
"What!? I have a sister in Israel?"
JK! JK!

The damn British soldiers. A great deal of energy and firepower went toward their removal from the region. I'd love to share some of what I heard, but as you know, sworn to secrecy . . .

bridge
British destroyed
agonizing screams
several dead

One of the Crazy 6—I can't name names—did something that landed him in prison. It was a temporary incarceration, though, because Mattityahu pressed hard for his release.

What alleged criminal act had him looking through bars at Promised Land Alcatraz? My apologies, but these chapped lips must remain sealed . . .

knife in stomach
neck chest
destroyed
again and again

Arabs came hard at the Jewish settlers, relentless in their attacks, determined to wipe out every *kibbutz* and village, children and women included. (To be clear, this is not a time jump to October 7, 2023, this attack occurred in 1947).

My father and others made sure the opposite occurred.

Sorry, I can't reveal what happened . . .

throats
knife fire
force Arabs
leave.

There are many more stories, of course, but the most riveting tales were never revealed, and they never will be. I've often wondered, though, what it was about his friend's grave site that got my father to open up, even that little bit. Israel is surreal, so maybe it wasn't my father doing the talking?

Never in my life have I called a psychic hotline, but based on the things we heard, I can't help but think it was Shlomo talking through my father, throwing his phantom voice, shrewdly using my father as a medium.

More than fifty years had passed since my father once again stepped foot onto the pioneering ground of Ramat Yohanan. Perhaps Shlomo just wanted to reminisce and share war stories like old soldiers do when they reunite after so many years.

Chinese Restaurant

FOSTER CITY, CALIFORNIA

Steve is pouring my father a cup of tea. I am nervously tapping a page in my notebook, because in my mind, I am un-redacting one of the incidents he unwittingly revealed to us while under the influence of Kibbutz Grave Pentothal, a powerful Schedule I drug. But as it tends to do, what happens in my mind, doesn't always stay in my mind . . .

TODD

So, Dad, about that retaliation for the assault on Jewish settlers, the one that you participated in, helped execute the plan . . .

The words cause my father to pull his teacup prematurely. Hot brown liquid stains cool white tablecloth. Steve looks at me as if I've lost my mind. I didn't, it just has lack of control issues.

DAD

What are you saying, schmuck?

TODD

Well, you shared a brief synopsis of the episode. I'm just envisioning a bit more detail, specifically your role in the attack.

DAD

I'd strongly suggest you shut this down. Now.

TODD

Okay, just stop me if I'm off . . . so you have this knife in your hand, a huge fucking blade sharpened just before the raid. You sneak up behind this armed guy and plunge the blade into his back—

DAD

Stop. I said stop. Now!

TODD

Nah, that doesn't seem like a David move. Bet it was more like . . . you sneak up behind this armed guy, aggressively wrap an arm around him and then drag the blade across his neck. Blood spurts and cascades down the victim's body.

My father's eyes widen; his face reddens. I'm just being a dick, but it seems I might be getting the story right. Fuck, I'm not sure I want to be right. I'm about to continue my imagined narrative, but then his face changes completely, going from level-3 rage to cocksure cool.

DAD

Really? Just the neck? Why stop there? You think I spent all that time sharpening my knife just to stop at the guy's neck?

When he's finished, a self-satisfied smile occupies the territory in the southern part of his face.

TODD

No way. Bullshit—are you playing me?

DAD

Hey Todd, can you grab me that menu over there? I've got a sudden craving for Rocky Mountain oysters in garlic sauce.

Over the decades, I've amassed enough indecorous and twisted experiences to fill a medium-sized storage unit of impropriety. I'd love to share some of these folktales with my kids before heading off to the big ad agency in the sky, but when I start to disclose stories from the lower end of the unsavory spectrum, they cover their ears and do that "lalalalalala, can't hear you," thing. So, for everyone's sake and sanity, it's probably best to keep most of these things redacted . . . for now, children. Who knows what kind of shit your Papa might drop if he ever gets around to writing another book.

Father vs. Sons

THE NOT-SO-GREAT-ISRAEL-PALESTINE-DEBATE

I, TOO, FOUGHT A WAR FOR INDEPENDENCE. THE YEAR WAS 1975. IT WAS a time of intense skirmishes, hostilities, and an escalation of expletives as I attempted to win freedom from a three-months-long grounding after being caught stealing cars (which I returned as close as possible to their original parking spaces).

A bit incongruous, for sure, but not so different from my high school buddy who'd pinch stuff from a 7-Eleven near our house but put it back on the shelf of another 7-Eleven a few blocks away—a calculated messing with the inventory game. Looking back, we followed the code of Gentlemen Thieves. Or perhaps it was the effects of some mushrooms. My motive? Did I even have one? A thrill? A rebellion? A wish to be seen as cool? Different? My father had a one-word definition: "schmuck." Perfect.

The conflict that almost took my father's life, on the other hand, well, that one is more complex, especially the aftermath and its dueling perspectives: Team Israel says their maneuvers are necessary for security. The other side says, "*Ya ahki* (c'mon man) this is apartheid." But let's not forget that they also say, "The river to the sea," which for me, used to describe how I viewed New York from the Hudson River to the Atlantic Ocean at Coney Island. Oh, and let's also never forget the Covenant of Hamas which calls for the *obliteration* of Israel and the *killing* of Jews. Talk about leaving a paper trail.

I used to see the situation solely through the Star of David prism, but I've also been willing to crane my neck to look beyond the stars.

And for this, my father has a three-word retort: "what-a-putzface."

Let's listen in on the debate that never ends . . .

TODD

Dad, I know you nearly lost your life, and they murdered your dearest friend, but can you at least try to see the anti-Zionist perspective?

1918 to 1948 . . . the British controlled what are now Israel, Gaza, and the West Bank. A little immigration here, a little immigration there. But then, after the war, a larger-scale Jewish immigration to the region. Naturally, the Palestinians were like, "Whoa, take it down a notch, cousins," and protested––okay, maybe not so peacefully––about what they considered an invasion.

STEVE

Jews should've taken a page from Emily Post, you know, bring a gift when visiting for the first time, like a *babka*.

DAD

Schmuck, whaddaya talking about visiting for the first time? Canaanites were there in the Bronze Age, for God's sake. Look, smart alecks—or should I say not-so-smart Todd and Steve—Jews have had religious and physical ties to the Land of Israel for thousands of years. Hyper-fast forward to 1947, and a Jewish homeland was sealed by the UN General Assembly, a decision enshrined in international law and by the spiritual law firm of Abraham, Moses, David & Solomon.

TODD

Or . . . seen through a different lens, an unwanted territory grab and the genesis for ongoing regional tension.

DAD

Woke putz say wha?

Guys, if you want to be progressive, then progress to the real story of the original victims—the Jews. The original underdogs—the Jews. Seriously, you say we need to see all sides, but lately, you and so many other "no-clue Jews" seem to have true-history cataracts.

Oh, the blur of naivety. Well, let's bring a few things into focus: Given the horror of twentieth-century antisemitism and the impossibility of Jewish survivors returning to the countries that annihilated them, there was simply no refuge anywhere in the world . . . other than our Palestine.

What's truly infuriating, is the perverse fact that the Holocaust created insufficient Western sympathy for Jews. Too many survivors were rejected by the US and Britain. So BACK to our ancestral home we go.

STEVE

No YIMBY?

DAD

What the hell kind of Jewspeak did they teach you morons in Hebrew school?

STEVE

No Yids In My Backyard.

DAD

Oh, of course, so obvious. How did I not get that? Maybe it's because I don't usually speak in idiotic acronyms. But I'll make an exception. Here, I got one:

PUTZ. P for putz, U for putz, T for putz, Z for putz.

Just when I thought I dodged his acronym bullet, my father glares at me.

DAD

Y for you too, O for you too, U for U too.

TODD

OUCH. Not an acronym guys, just absorbing the hit. Yeah, Dad, it's shameful. But the people in Palestine bore no responsibility for the Holocaust, and now they were responsible for taking Jews in?

DAD

Hmm, perhaps if we lost a million additional souls, a cool seven million deaths instead of six million, maybe other parts of the world would have embraced us after such immense tragedy? Remember that the next time that you half-educated half-wits participate in an anti-Israel march.

STEVE

Don't forget your *keffiyeh*, Todd. It could get cold out there.

DAD

Zionism was a movement of national salvation. Jewish immigrants to Palestine had a spiritual connection to the holy land they entered. Let me correct that . . . *re-entered*. We were in the sandbox first.

Also, Jews did not seize local property. They paid handsomely for it.

STEVE

Holy Zillow! Can you imagine the haggling between a Jew and an Arab during a property sale negotiation?

TODD

Far from an equitable split, though. In 1947, the UN voted to give the Jews 55 percent of the land for an independent state, while the Arabs got the rest. And the rest is bloody history.

DAD

Bubeleh, the 1947 plan to divide Palestine into Jewish and Arab states was not equitable because most of the land awarded to the Jews was barren desert. Which we turned green by defending our ploughshares with our swords.

TODD

Yet in the ensuing war, Jews not only seized more of Palestine but used the fighting as a pretext to execute a program of expansionism.

DAD

DEFENSIVE EXPANSIONISM, you *pisher*.

Never forget that they will never acknowledge our right to exist, and many pray daily to wipe us off the face of the earth. My partially educated and misguided son, the failure to create an independent Palestinian state reflected not Jewish aggression but chronically deficient Palestinian leadership.

Palestinians view themselves as victims. But the fact is, they decided violence trumps negotiations. Had they accepted in 1937 or 1947 the partition plans, a Palestinian state might have been established decades ago.

Do me a favor, in between projecting those puerile and demagogic anti-Israel slogans onto buildings, have your self-loathing Jew buddies do a little digging beyond their social media bullshit, and they might actually learn something—like the fact that any level of occupation grew directly from the Arabs' 1967 military effort, eagerly supported by Palestinians to destroy Israel. Without that assault, Israel would not have seized the West Bank, Gaza, or Golan Heights. Again, DEFENSIVE EXPANSIONISM. And speaking of defense, do you think Israel would exist without an Iron Dome, an ingenious DEFENSIVE weapon? You see the theme here, schmuck?

TODD

Okay, I get it. And I get the moral narrative of Jews returning to the only place that would take them and the disgrace that so many battered survivors were turned away rather than welcomed with open hearts and open arms. But will there ever come a time of a "reasonable" compromise?

DAD

Plenty of genuinely good attempts have been made. Look back to 2000 when Bill Clinton proposed a compromise that would have returned 97 percent of the occupied territories to an independent Palestinian state.

STEVE

Arafat didn't say yes to the redress.

DAD

Sadly, no. He rejected Clinton's "Hail Mary" proposal and then sanctioned a terrorist campaign that created years of toxic distrust.

STEVE

Proving that American football language, especially phrases featuring the mother of Jesus, might not be the best way to resolve regional conflicts.

DAD

Now hear this, sailors: In 2005, Israel gave it another go and unilaterally left Gaza, another serious attempt to settle down the tensions. "Thanks a lot, bomb you later," said Hamas and subsequently used the territory to launch thousands of missiles at the Israelis.

TODD

Sure, but then why do the United Nations and other international human rights organizations still consider the Gaza Strip to be under military occupation, with control over air and maritime space, basic needs like utilities, transportation, water, communications and—

STEVE

And on and on and on and on. Enough, can we please call a ceasefire?

DAD

We had one, boys, up until October 7 of '23. Can you guess who broke it? Look, like it or not, I am spiritually and historically tethered to the Israeli narrative, and as a result, feel an obligation to continually defend what I fought to defend. I do wish both sides could recognize one another and finally be free and independent after so many wounding years.

STEVE

Wow, that's the most generous and empathetic thing I've heard you say on the subject. Todd, any closing remarks?

TODD

It's a lot to absorb. Regardless of where your allegiances lie in this wobbly region of the world, it's worth taking a crash course in perspective. There's plenty of galvanizing as well as divisive information from both sides of the graffiti-covered wall, that impermeable barrier between two contingents whose eye-for-an-eye values will forever prevent them from seeing eye-to-eye.

Shalom, brothers and sisters.
Asalaamu alaikum, cousins.
May peace be with you.

Electchester Apartments, Queens

EARLY 1970s

MY FATHER HAD AT LEAST A DOZEN BULLETS IN HIS NIGHTSTAND. I CAME upon this .38-caliber discovery in my search for a pair of socks. I was out of socks, so I went on the hunt in my parents' bedroom, opening random drawers, even ones I knew would not yield anything to cover my feet. I thought, *Heck, while I'm here, I might as well dig around, see what else turns up.*

Well, well . . . a velvet pouch filled with silver dollars appeared. It was attempting to conceal a pornographic paperback. The book contained a slim section of nasty black and white photos—apparently they were critical to illustrating the narrative. It was a well-worn book, its XXX images coming apart from the spine of the "novel." I've read that book more times than I've read *The Great Gatsby*, and I read Gatz a lot. But time was short, and I didn't want to get caught. So, we beat on (or was it off?) boats against the current, borne back ceaselessly into the past and present of my parents' stuff.

Opening their closet door revealed additional artifacts: a box of home movies and the 8mm projector used for viewings. There was another box of 8mm films with titles similar to the paperback novel I'd stumbled upon just a few minutes earlier. Clearly, my parents were open-minded, probably one degree away from swingers. I've never asked; I never want to know.

I also found an accordion folder that held important documents including bank statements, receipts, and expired warranties. If I had dug around in that folder a bit more, I would have put my hands on a fake ID—the one with a swastika on the cover and, on the inside, a picture of my father as a young kid but with a different name than the one on his birth certificate. I was so close. But my hand went in a different direction and grabbed a small white envelope instead.

Ooh, such beautiful treasure this was. Hello ladies! A dark-haired woman, a tall blonde woman, a woman laying across the hood of a car, a woman in a big fur hat, two women with very large breasts, a dark-skinned woman holding a little dog, and a photo of my mom in a bathing suit; so make that *three* women with very large breasts.

There was also a woman dressed as a soldier—an Israeli soldier.

Feeling that I had exhausted the bedroom closet research, I moved my investigation to the dusty world under their bed. Turns out, nothing to see here, folks.

So, I got back on my feet and pulled open a few more drawers, but again, nothing worth mentioning.

In movies, I had seen how people hide money under their mattresses, so the next thing I did was slide my hand into the space between the box spring and mattress. *Eureka!* On my mother's side of the bed was a stack of bills, at least $200. I helped myself to a tenner. I walked over to my father's side of the bed, reached under the mattress, and felt something cold and metal. Without lifting the mattress, I knew it was a gun.

I suppose it could've been an adult toy, but really, I was 99 percent certain it was a gun and not an object that vibrated. Yep, it was a .38-caliber handgun. Cool, and perfectly understandable since my father and his business partner, Ted, owned a pharmacy in Manhattan on 34th Street, just a short distance from Macy's and Madison Square Garden. How about that for coming full circle? He was still involved in the drug trade, but this time around, it was kosher. He now had a proper business license. No need to stash medications in a hidden trouser pocket.

I was sitting on the floor, studying the gun carefully, it was heavier than I had imagined. Suddenly, the door to the room where my parents slept (and God knows what else) burst open. Shit, shit, my brother! Thankfully, I was a crouching ninja concealed at the far end of the bed, imperceptible to Steve. Hmm, what was he doing in here? Seems I wasn't the only inquisitive hunter out there on the Plains of the Parents' Bedroom.

Like a hippo in a river, my eyes protruded from the top of the mattress while the rest of my head and body remained submerged. I could see Steve knew exactly what big game he was after, going straight for the drawer that contained the silver dollars and the great American illustrated porn novel. But unlike my rookie moves, he cautiously lifted and shifted the contents in that drawer without leaving any trace of disturbance, steady as a specialist who defuses landmines. From my just-below-mattress vantage point, I could see Steve was growing frustrated, the need for teenage release, hoowee, it can drive a young man crazy. Which, truth be told, is why I ran out of socks . . .

Okay, I made the decision to be a cool brother, one who'd covertly figure out a way to get Steve the material he so desperately needed. My plan? Crawl under my parents' bed to the other side, then silently reach up and slip the book next to the lamp on my mom's nightstand. Porn in plain sight. Sure, he'd be shocked to discover that our mom might be reading a book that wasn't borrowed from the Queensborough Public Library, but considering the frenzy in his pants, I figured he wouldn't give it too much thought.

And so, the good brother swings into action. I nimbly . . .

Fuck no, are you fucking kidding me? Did you think I'd throw away my shot at gotcha glory?

Hippo rapidly ascends from the murky blue river of shag carpet, hoists the dirty paperback in the air and ejaculates the words, "LOOKING FOR THIS, MOTHERFUCKER?"

Good thing my brother was an athlete with a strong heart, because he fell backward clutching his chest. His recovery, it should be noted, was swift. Rather than yell or throw punches, all he said was, "You're an asshole. Now give me the book; you're too young to be looking at that kind of stuff," as he walked over to take it from my hand. And that's when he saw what was in my other hand—my father's gun. So, being an overprotective brother, he slapped me with the book; *BAM*, a *Hot Sucker* punch to the face! Better than a pistol whipping, I suppose, but that shit hurt, and it was not about to go unanswered. Instantly, my parents bed became a wrestling ring. The match? Pedro Morales vs. Bruno Sammartino, our favorite wrestlers at the time, and we went at it hard: Bodyslams, Atomic Spinecrushers, Lariats. My brother's size was a distinct advantage over my speed, so in under three minutes, I found myself pinned to the mat(tress).

Steve boastfully began counting aloud: 1 . . . 2 . . . 3 . . .

We break. Steve, the victor, raises the pornographic novel over his head—a stand-in for the championship wrestling belt. I take the gun and pretend I'm going to shoot myself for losing the match, and that's when the universe turned on The Brothers Diamond. Because who should be standing at the entrance to the bedroom? One of its primary occupants.

Man, what our poor Papa saw: one schmucky son holding a dirty book, the other biological disappointment waving a gun around. Look, you can breathe easy, the gun was not loaded. But my dad's fists sure were. They were locked, cocked, and fully loaded with the wrestler Ox Baker's signature knockout move, The Heart Punch. BAM! BAM! Trust Issues Smackdown!

We both fell hard. My father was so sickened and thoroughly fed up with our behavior that he simply walked away spewing a string of acidic-sounding Yiddish words that neither of us had ever heard before.

Now, back to that gun.

The early seventies was not the safest time in New York City's history. Selling pharmaceuticals meant you needed protection. A gun was necessary, and sensible. As a matter of fact, on two separate occasions, armed robbers had the opportunity to look straight into the barrel of my father's gun. No shots were fired. The suspects fled without a single pill or a single drop of cough syrup.

His gun wasn't the only protection I ferreted out in the hunt for socks. Putting two plus two plus .38 together, I pulled open the drawer of my father's nightstand expecting to find the bullets. They were there, all right. So were the socks—nylon foot protection. But I also chanced upon the largest cache of condoms I'd ever seen in my life. I'd struck latex gold. Ramses was the brand.

It's either a two-headed irony or a two-fisted coincidence: First off, the fact that my father, decades after smuggling drugs into the Ghetto for my grandfather's patients, ends up owning a pharmacy and dispensing drugs . . . legitimately. If you are wondering whether my father and his partner, along with their pharmacist, sampled any of the more popular drugs at the time like Quaaludes, the answer is yes. They got 'luded, they got speedy, and they got Valium'd too.

And for good measure, my father got high on more organic substances. How do I know this? It was New Year's Eve, near the end of the seventies:

"Hey, Dad, before I head out to the party, do you want to get high?"

He put up a fuss saying he'd never do that; drugs are bad, dope is for dopes, you know, all the things a parent should say when asked such a question. I was relentless. "Come on, Dad, it's New Year's Eve, I really want this father-son-sativa bonding moment."

He relented. "Sure, why not, but just so you know, I've never smoked marijuana before," he told me.

My father suggested we go to my bedroom, close the door, open the window, and never say anything about it to my mother. "Deal," I excitedly replied. I fired up the bowl and passed the pipe to my father. He put his lips to the pipe, covered the bowl with his hand, inhaled deeply and deftly lifted his palm, shooting the smoke deep into his lungs. He held it there for a long time, then exhaled . . . out the window, of course.

"Whoa, dude, and not a single cough," I observed in a stunned stoner-voice. "That is some professional-level smoking skill."

Before I could get any other stoner expressions out, he said, "Don't look so surprised, I go to a lot of trade shows."

And then, there's those Ramses brand condoms. Really, Dad? Did you not see Yul Brynner in the *Ten Commandments* at least ten times? Are you not familiar with the Eleventh Commandment: *Thou Shalt Not Roll onto Thy Dick Condoms Named for an Enslaver of the Jewish People?* Not only that, but Ramses also purportedly sired over one hundred children, which should have caused you to question their effectiveness.

34th Street, Manhattan

EARLY 1970s

WHAT THE MAYOR OF NEW YORK CITY SHOULD HAVE DONE WAS PRESENT a public health award to my father and his business partner. Their pharmacy was located right next door to one of the most notorious brothels in all of Manhattan (a truly high-class lust establishment). So naturally, his store was the most convenient place for gentleman to procure their condoms. Also, breath mints, just in case the lovely lady selected for the one-hour date wanted to kiss them on the mouth.

A few years ago, I took my father on a trip to New York City. We made a special visit to the former location of his pharmacy. It's now a Gap Store. Standing there on 34th street summoned a flood of memories from his entrepreneurial past. But surprise, the thing I was most interested in was not his stories about hard work and profits. Please, Father, please give me some bawdy tales of the tails next door who worked hard for the money . . .

"So you want to know what kind of guys stopped into my store before heading up to the brothel?" my father asked as he looked up and down the block, checking to see if anyone was listening.

"Yeah, Dad. I think it'd make an interesting detail for your book."

"Okay, well, one of my favorite customers, and a regular client of the brothel, was a boorish guy with a toupee named Manny. Ah, good ol' horny Manny; he'd come into the store to purchase a jar of Albolene moisturizing cream right before heading to the twenty-third floor of the hotel. The reason? If you're squeamish, Son, I can skip the details."

"No, no, please continue. I can take it."

"Well, after he selected his date for the hour, Manny would remove his hairpiece—he was totally bald—and then rub a glob of Albolene all over his head before using his noggin' for the nookie, spiraling left, whirling to the right, and boring straight into the tunnel. He swore up and down to me that his special methods never failed to bring his lady to climax."

"Now that's a beautiful story, Dad. Tantric sex masters could learn a thing or two from that guy."

What an outstanding public service their pharmacy was performing, keeping working men and sex workers safe from catching or spreading any bad stuff. The McAlpin Hotel was also the preferred layover spot for airline pilots and stewardesses. Apparently, those who flew the friendly skies were indeed very friendly and lived up to all the stereotypes regarding the profession's promiscuity.

Now, I'm no math genius, but if you add sex workers + horny men from the boroughs + philanderers from the 'burbs + airline pilots + flight crews + local politicians + visiting celebrities, you get a pharmacy that sold more Ramses brand condoms than any other pharmacy in the entire country.

In the end, it's okay that they didn't receive a well-deserved certificate of merit from His Honor, Mayor John Lindsay, because they attained something even better: their sheathing achievements won each of them all-expenses-paid trips to Europe, compliments of Ramses.

Bon voyage, Dynamic Rubber Duo.

One more thing: You don't become the undisputed condom champion of the country without a critical person in your corner—someone who believes in you and trusts you with $50,000 of her hard-earned dollars.

Her name was Iamnot Telling. (See what I did there? My dad swore me to secrecy.) How my father knew the brothel's madam and why she'd be willing to personally loan him $50,000 to buy an equal share of the pharmacy business remains a mystery to me.

He insists it's because of all the clients he sent her way. But as we stood outside the place that once brought so much pleasure to the city that never sleeps (without a condom, thanks to my father), I once again pressed him on the matter. He just said, "Don't be a schmuck. She was a friend. I helped her, she helped me. Enough said."

"Sorry, Dad. Not buying it," I skeptically replied.

"Not buying . . . you're not thinking straight, Todd."

"I'll tell you what I'm thinking. I'm thinking that you and the madam had a very special relationship, one that involved some kinky role playing."

"There he goes again, the imagination on this fucking kid."

"Oh, touched the cavernous penile nerve, did I?"

"Uh, you're just being a dick."

"I'm picturing it now. You're in her hotel suite. The madam emerges from behind a privacy screen dressed as a shepherdess, looking exactly like the farmer's daughter from Germany. She throws you onto a pile of hay and roughly 'takes your virginity.' I bet this happened about once a month. Right, Dad?"

"You almost got it right, Son. There was also a couple of sheep involved."

His business partner, Ted, had seed money from his mother. My dad was self-made, but he hadn't fully made it yet. Whatever the reason, be it sordid or noble, the madam's funding ensured my immigrant father got a bigger slice of The Big Apple pie.

Chinese Restaurant

FOSTER CITY, CALIFORNIA

I refill my father's teacup, but only a quarter of the way. I want to keep him at the table, not in the bathroom.

TODD

I have another question for you. The brothel. Was it right next door to your pharmacy or on another street nearby?

DAD

Next door, twenty-third floor of the McAlpin Hotel. It's apartments now. Condoms, I think.

TODD

You meant to say condos, right?

DAD

Right.

I goaded him hard about his close relationship with the madam. Back in the day, $50,000 was a small fortune. Why would she take such a financial risk on an immigrant? Did my father have a unique, highly desirable penis from all that reverse circumcision stuff? I also wondered if there was ever a time when I could have been calling the madam, Madam Mommy. But when pressed on the question, he always responded with this exact phrase, like a programmed Jewbot: "Don't be a schmuck. She was a friend. I helped her, she helped me. Enough said."

Electchester Apartments, Queens

LATE 1970s

OKAY, SO MAYBE IT'S NOT AS COOL AS HAVING A FAMOUS MADAM TO CALL Mommy, but at least the woman who married my father was a truly progressive Brooklyn broad.

See, I learned that my parents have two anniversary dates; one is their celebrated wedding date which featured a party and guests handing over greeting cards stuffed with American dollars.

The other, the wedding date that occurred several months prior to the wedding party, celebrates the blessed occasion of . . . a pregnancy scare.

My mom was late and my parents panicked, so they rushed to City Hall along with my mom's parents as witnesses and tied the knot. A couple of things: Even though they were conservative Jews, my mom's parents were fine with the situation. They had no issue with sex before marriage. Come to think of it, my grandfather was a card-carrying member of the Communist party—perhaps that explains the liberal attitudes. Second, how amazing to find out that my mom wasn't a virgin when she got married.

Museum of Modern Art Manhattan

EARLY 1970s

DECADES BEFORE WE VISITED THE ISRAELI SITES OF WAR AND THE DEATH camp Treblinka, my father dragged me to another bloodied battleground. It was in a museum. He grabbed me by the arm, rather forcefully, and placed me directly in the line of fire of *Guernica*.

"I want you to look at it, all of it, then tell me what you think," he demanded. He kept his eyes on me as I gave the enormous painting a once-over. What, exactly, was my father trying to accomplish? It's not like he was an art lover; rarely did we go to galleries or museums. In fact, we had a total of five pieces of art in our apartment: an oil painting of a rabbi (he still has it and insists it's worth a fortune; it is not). Also, a painting of a seascape and three small pictures of topless women. Those last three aren't even paintings; they're trivets, and they hung in our bathroom above the toilet. You could press a scalding cup of hot chocolate against those perky breasts while taking a leak and not damage the heat-resistant masterpieces.

As I recall, Picasso's war-torn canvas hung on a wall all by itself. No surprise. I mean, come on, what other painting would want to be in the vicinity of such a violent downer? I wasn't thrilled about this part of our father-son culture excursion. Look, if I'm getting dragged to a museum—a museum without any dinosaur bones—then I wish to see certain things, like paintings of naked women. Honestly, I really was expecting a highfalutin sex education lesson: "The Talk" vividly delivered via Boobs Throughout the Ages. Instead, I was getting an introduction to the history of war, my father's second or third favorite subject. Sex, if you haven't figured out by now, is definitely in his top three, which is why I thought this museum jaunt would be providing plenty to think about as I tried to fall asleep that night.

Guernica was dreary, nothing like the paintings on nearby walls in gilded frames. Or the painting that really upset my father—a giant square of one solid color. I also heard there was a super-cool painting in the museum. Supposedly, the artist used his dick as a paintbrush. *Where's that? Take me to see that one, Father.* Because this thing that I was staring at was nothing but bleak black, bleak gray, and bleak white, the color of the snow outside of the museum—once white snow that had been rolled over by a thousand yellow taxis. This painting was so bland, refusing to absorb or reflect any wavelengths of light from the violet/blue end of the spectrum.

Seriously, how is this a war painting? I was watching war almost every night on our new color TV, disturbing images beamed in from jungles. The war I saw was red; it wore blood-soaked bandages. War had painted faces; shades of jungle green. It was golden brown; thatched roofs in remote villages bursting into brilliant flames of yellow and orange.

And Agent Orange.

Fuck this. This is ugly and boring. I attempted to flee the war zone.

"Not so fast," my father sternly museum-whispered as he shoved me back into the trench. He then delivered a sixty-second briefing on how Guernica was bombed by Nazi Luftwaffe planes during the Spanish Civil War. Okay, that made it a little more interesting. But who wants to stare at a painting with such little color? I looked back at my father.

He was not fucking around; he was dead serious. So, I gave in. I looked at it. Really looked. And I had to take a step closer. My eyes locked eyes with a toppled face in the corner of the painting. The eyes seemed dead. I looked up, and there was an unflinching bull and a screaming woman, maybe a mother. And there was another upside-down person, maybe her child. By the look of its eyes, also dead. And there were so many severed arms with busted hands clinging to busted weapons. And harsh edges that seemed to grab your gaze and take it to the next place and then the next place. Flashes of light that kept lifting your eyes all the way up, up, until they crashed into that poor horse; for crying out loud, a crying out horse—a terrified beast caught in the middle of . . . war.

All righty, that was intense, but now, back to Mission Titties. I turned to make my way to the "fine" art, but I hit an obstacle: my father. He was directly behind me the whole time, anticipating an attempted getaway.

"Let's see if you were paying attention. Tell me when the bombing of Guernica happened," he said firmly.

"Well, it being black and white, like the old movies you make me watch, I'm gonna say . . . 1930s-ish?"

"Putz, it was 1937. And do you know what happened two years after that?" he asked.

"Hmm, Technicolor came to cinema, but probably not to paintings by Picasso," was my wiseass response.

"The Nazis bombed Warsaw, my city. God, how did I raise such an—"

"Dad, I'm not a whatever-you're-about-to-call-me . . . a putz, a *mamzer, a schlimazel, a nudnik, a schlub* . . . I get it, war sucks. It's horror and chaos. If it makes you feel any better, I couldn't sleep for weeks after reading *All Quiet on the Western Front.* Another book I read, *Johnny Got His Gun,* fucked with my head. And *Slaughterhouse Five*? Completely blew my mind, literally surreal, the relentless bombing and flattening of Dresden, the trauma, the firestorms—tens of thousands of people incinerated. I promise you, I get it, but I just really, really want to see, you know . . . other stuff."

"Okay, Son. Go off and look at all the nudes that your feeble little mind can take in."

"Right on, Dad. Thanks; see you later."

"Meet me at the entrance in exactly one hour," he ordered. And then under his breath he muttered, "You foolish little *pisher.*"

As hard as it was to be released from the art of war discussion and my father's interrogation, I finally managed to escape the anguish and heartbreak of *Guernica*. To hell with that Hell. Hell, I was in The Modern, and I was on a mission. I stepped back, way back, and scouted the art-filled walls. I was determined to find some paintings of naked ladies.

According to my father, this was a test to determine if I was mature enough to receive his story about the war. I failed. He'd have to wait a few more years.

Chinese Restaurant

FOSTER CITY, CALIFORNIA

My father is growing impatient; he is slowly and rhythmically stabbing the table with a chopstick.

TODD

You ready for that dessert, Dad? And were you just tapping out Hatikvah?

DAD

Good ear, and yeah, how long does it take to slice a few crappy non-Jaffa oranges? What are they doing back there, baking the cake?

TODD

I was talking about the other dessert. You know, the final course. You said you'd talk about our visit there . . . for the book.

He clearly isn't getting the cryptic speak. Steve steps in to help.

STEVE

Okay, Dad, here's a clue. If this was an Italian restaurant that served Holocaust-themed desserts, Todd would be ordering . . . Tirablinkamisu.

TODD

Yeah, Dad, dark and bittersweet.

My father polishes off his scotch. He is still not tracking with his son's indirect query. He's about to speak, but just then, dessert arrives. I quickly grab a fortune cookie.

TODD

Says here, 'You will help finish Todd's book by talking about the time your sons took you to Treblinka. And then you will spill your guts about everything that happened in Israel.'

DAD

Ahh, now I see. Okay, you want me to shed a few tears about Treblinka? Fine. But Israel? Keep dreaming, Son.

Treblinka, Poland

EARLY 1940s

ON THE WEBSITE *DARK TOURISM*, THE TREBLINKA DEATH CAMP RECEIVES a "darkometer" rating of 9. Seriously? A 9? How did we not receive a perfect score? Before challenging the judges, I looked a little deeper into the website and quickly discovered a couple of destinations that did earn the coveted "darkometer" score of 10. The first was Hiroshima. The other, not surprisingly, was Auschwitz. I do appreciate the work of the site's curators. I imagine it's comparable to the work being done by Facebook content moderators—the ones who sued for damages caused by the psychological trauma incurred after reviewing copious amounts of violent and graphic images.

I wanted to explore the site further—a few more clicks may well have revealed some additional perfect 10s (and horrific 9s)—but whoa, I had to tap out. I'm a dark individual, but I have limits. I'm just dark-curious.

Hear me out, judges. Perhaps we can split the difference on the unsung and rarely visited Treblinka and raise the score to a darkly respectable 9.5? Because quantitatively speaking, it's pretty close to the tally of the death camp that receives more than a million living visitors annually:

> Auschwitz: 1.1 million deaths, eight gas chambers, plus one Josef Mengele.

> Treblinka: 900,000 deaths, two gas chambers, plus one Ivan "the Terrible" Marchenko.

But I get it, when you look closely at the stats (bonus points for Mengele), Auschwitz clearly deserves to be the darkest of the dark. For my family, though, Treblinka is Vantablack, one of the darkest substances known, absorbing up to 99.965 percent of visible light.

Another important difference between the reigning champion of darkness and Treblinka––the silver medalist of death camps––is that Auschwitz leaves little to the imagination. For the most part, the Nazis left things in their original condition when they abandoned it at the end of the war. To this day, substantial evidence of systematic mass murder abounds, including watchtowers, railway ramps, barbed-wire fences, the crematoriums, the deceptive *Arbeit Macht Frei* welcome sign, prison barracks, and gas chambers. There's all that, plus the infamous piles and mounds of shoes, human hair, suitcases, and eyeglasses.

Visitors should appreciate how those provocative artifacts of atrocity are soberly displayed and not overly stylized. It forces serious contemplation about complicity and the precipitous disappearance of humanity.

Treblinka, on the other hand, offers a minimalist experience. Minimalist in the sense that almost nothing remains. The camp was such a next-level death factory, the Nazis had to destroy the evidence, leave no trace.

In 1943, as things were falling apart, the Nazis tore it apart, burned it down, spit on it, cursed at it, and got the hell out of the Hell that they'd created. Turns out, though, the Nazis were far less efficient at cover-up then they were at genocide. Buildings and other structures were pulverized into tiny fragments, but the crime-scene cleanup proved to be more challenging, especially in their attempt to camouflage mass graves. The Nazis used what they had at their disposal—a perverse cocktail of soil and human ashes stirred, shaken, and combined to conceal the expansive killing grounds.

It almost worked.

For several decades, survivor stories, artworks, and the occasional Nazi journal that turned up painted a vivid picture of Treblinka's infrastructure and the savagery that occurred beyond the walls and wire. Recently, however, some of what was trapped only in imagination came to life.

Archaeological excavations at Treblinka, led by Caroline Sturdy Colls, a forensic archaeologist who collaborates with detectives to find murder victims, identified new mass graves (the largest being sixty-three feet by fifty-eight feet as revealed by LIDAR). Human bones damaged by acts of torture were discovered throughout the area. They were quickly returned to the earth. Jewish rabbinical law prohibits the disturbance of grave sites.

The excavations also uncovered two sets of gas chambers at Treblinka. The first had a capacity of about 600 people; the second accommodated 5,000. Unlike in Auschwitz, Zyklon B was not used as the primary agent of death. At Treblinka, the gas chambers were pumped full of exhaust from military tank engines. Less efficient, perhaps, but it got the job done. Come to think of it, if Zyklon B had been deployed there, might Treblinka have edged out Auschwitz in death count . . . ?

Based on additional maddening research, it wouldn't surprise me if the craftier Nazis escaped to America after the war and found gigs as Hollywood set designers or headlined as illusionists on the Las Vegas Strip. The visual effects created by the architects of infernos were terribly convincing.

Their meticulous deceit began with informing Jews they were going to a transit camp before beginning a new life in a different part of Eastern Europe. And talk about attention to detail: the Nazis constructed a fake train station complete with a false ticket booth including posted train schedules and a clock with fake hands painted on it.

If those imagined hands had been attached to actual Swiss watch movements, less than one hour would pass between the moment Jews dropped their belongings, stripped out of their clothes, and walked into the fumes that would consume them.

If that phony clock had kept real time, twenty damned minutes would pass before 5,000 people inside the gas chambers collapsed onto illusory tiles, flattened by carbon monoxide. Many would die standing upright—the bodies were pressed so tightly together that there was no chance to fall. The orange tiles excavated by the archaeologists matched eyewitness accounts of the gas chamber floors.

Chillingly, each tile was stamped with a Star of David, likely part of the Nazi subterfuge that the building was a Jewish-style bathhouse.

How's this for a final design flourish: a large Star of David was placed at the top of a building facing the camp to create the appearance of an old-fashioned synagogue. When the construction was finished, the *Hauptsturmfuhrer* said to his subordinates, "The Jew-town has been completed at last."

And since every mass extermination needs a soothing soundtrack, the reception area featured an orchestra that welcomed the unsuspecting prisoners with joyful music: prelude to a requiem.

Treblinka had a single function—to kill. In a standard workday (plus unpaid overtime), 12,000 to 15,000 people were murdered. Large cremation pits were constructed to incinerate the gassed bodies. Frankly, it was shoddy engineering by German standards—basically, the pits had blocks of concrete at the base. On top of that, wood was placed, and on top of that were railroad ties, forming a grate. And to top it all off, bodies were thrown onto the grates and splashed with petrol to accelerate the burn.

One survivor, Jankiel Wiernik, an eyewitness to the flaming horror, noted how the bellies of pregnant women exploded from boiling amniotic fluid.

So, how's that 9.5 score looking now?

Exactly how does a Third Reich efficiently scale mayhem and murder? With an organizational chart and the threat of death, of course.

Jewish prisoners were broken into several teams called *Sonderkommando* squads. Since knit shirts emblazoned with company logos weren't available at the time, each squad had a different colored triangle. There was the blue unit (*Kommando Blau*) which managed the rail ramp and unlocked the freight wagons. They'd greet the new arrivals and haul out those who had died in transit. They also removed personal belongings and were forced to clean the human sorrow that clung to the wagon floors.

The red unit (*Kommando Rot*) was the largest squad. Their job was to unpack and sort the belongings of victims after they had been *processed*. (Himmler thought the word "annihilation" was too strong a term, so he softened it by insisting on more friendly final-solution business jargon.)

After they got the goods, the red squad moved the precious family possessions to the storage barracks, which were managed by the yellow squad (*Kommando Gelb*). This team's responsibilities included separating the items by quality, carefully removing the Star of David from garments and clipping sewn threads to extract money that was hidden in the lining of clothing.

The yellow unit was followed by the *Desinfektionskommando*; their job was to disinfect everything from household items to the sacks of hair from murdered women.

A level higher on the org chart was the *Goldjuden* unit or "Gold Jews." They collected and counted the banknotes and appraised the gold and jewelry. In addition to that cushy Jewish stereotype of a job, there were other work details near the top of the org chart that had no interaction with prison transports. These included the *Holzfällerkommando* (woodcutter unit) who made sure there was always enough wood for the human bonfires.

The *Tarnungskommando* (disguise unit) spruced up the place by camouflaging the structures of death. And then, the job that everyone wanted when they spun the wheel of chores: simply cleaning the common areas.

Now, let's drop way down in the org chart. Here you find a group of approximately 300 men called the *Totenjuden* ("Jews of death"). These unfortunate souls lived across from the gas chambers. Their duties included taking corpses to the pits for cremation after gold teeth had been extracted. This shit work gets shittier; they were also responsible for keeping the pyres burning, crushing the remaining bones, and collecting ashes for disposal.

Although each squad had a different team color, they all shared one thing in common—continuous beatings by the guards until the inevitable moment, usually just a few days later, when they'd be shot and replaced by new arrivals.

Now, if you'll kindly allow me to continue the campaign for a darkometer 9.5 score . . . Remember that camp guard, Ivan the Terrible? Well, apparently, gassing and incinerating humans just wasn't enough for him (it was probably a dopamine deficiency). In addition to leading the mass extermination process, he was also a do-it-yourselfer who would torture, beat, and kill with his gloved hands. Sometimes he'd use tools like metal pipes to split heads open, break out a sword to impale his victims, or reach for a bayonet to slice off noses and ears as well as gouge out eyes.

I hope you agree that I've made a compelling case for reconsideration. However, my petition for an adjustment to Treblinka's ghastliness recognition doesn't end there.

Calibrators of the "darkometer," get ready to recast your votes.

Several survivors testified that Ivan killed countless infants by bashing them against a wall, typically skull first. Apparently, Ivan was a role model because his degree of brutality was practiced by other camp guards who were awed by his handiwork. Some even got it into their heads to rip an infant child from a mother's arms, turn the child upside down, and then tear the child in half by their tiny legs.

What? Were there no Yellow Pages phone books available to demonstrate their machismo? Also, the sickening move of snatching the living, breathing, crying infants and tossing them directly into the flames was a regular method of human disposal.

Here's one more for the records: Witnesses claimed that Ivan raped young girls before cutting their abdomens open and letting them bleed to death. Did he think that would drain his precious semen? Clearly, that bedlamite needed a lesson in female anatomy. Of course, there are many more examples. The problem is, so few survivors remain to tell these stories. In fact, fewer than seventy people made it out of Treblinka. They were severely damaged, but alive.

Researching Treblinka is especially hard. There are several revolting eyewitness reports, but not only that—it's personal. Which is why I keep placing my grandfather into every dispiriting scene I read about. I hang onto the hope that a survivor will blurt out his name and gush about what a good doctor he was, how, without flinching, he'd help patch up a face that had been hacked apart by a Nazi dagger and then nonchalantly say, "Next patient, please."

For example, in Jankiel Wiernik's detailed account called *A Year in Treblinka*, he writes:

> About that time, I caught a cold, which developed into pneumonia. All of the sick were being killed either by shooting or by injections, but it seems that the Germans needed me. Accordingly, they gave me whatever medical attention was available. A Jewish physician attended me, examined me every day, and gave me medicine and comfort.

And his name was . . . ? Come on, Jankiel, a name! What was the physician's name? Did he mention that he had a son who smuggled medicines into the Warsaw Ghetto for him so he could keep treating patients, putting his own life at risk to help others?

Anything, Jankiel, please. *Please.*

Jankiel's agonizing telling of his time in Treblinka includes many names, but not the name of the physician who helped him. Therefore, I believe I have the right to insert a name of my choosing into the blank space left by Jankiel. I will write the name and profession of my grandfather, Izrael Diamenstein, Dr n. Med: Doktor Nauk Medycznych.

Eyewitness accounts, especially the explicit reports from Jankiel Wiernik, are unsparing. You sob while reading the stories. They are repugnant to the point where I needed a vomit bag, but who keeps a vomit bag handy? Thankfully, my desk is on a concrete floor, so the cleanup wasn't too bad.

It's extremely hard to read through so much unsettling material. However, every now and then, you come across a few words about resistance—heroic tales about Jews who stood up to the killers and psychopaths. No way were they sticking around, suppliantly waiting for a Stan Lee superhero to swoop in and save the day: It's MessiahMan! More powerful than a speeding locomotive pulling fifty cattle cars. MessiahMan! Able to bend barbed wire with his bare hands.

I can't speak for my grandfather, but I know my father rejected any mesmerizing Jewish fairy tale.

Fortunately, there were others like him who contemptuously said, "That's *meshuggah*." Nervy and defiant, these rebels would never be paralyzed by fear or a savior fantasy; they were emboldened to take matters of survival into their own hands.

The odds against the defiant few were stacked higher than a Nazi guard watchtower, and yet, some of these depleted men and women managed to defy the dreadful conditions of the death camp, enjoy a long life, raise families, and when ready, recount their personal horrors and suffering. These include Chil Rajchman, author of *The Last Jew of Treblinka*, a survivor who believed the bravest thing one can do is to remember and share what you witnessed. And Jankiel Wiernik's accounts are brutally straightforward descriptions of the horrors, but also stories about resistance and escape. These are the inspiring tales that lifted me—a kind of Holocaust research sorbet—a few moments of light in the unbearable darkness of history.

Regrettably, light is once again being eclipsed by recent events across college campuses. If only these passionate, albeit asymmetrically informed students had a deeper understanding of certain dates that preceded October 7, 2023, perhaps they might reconceptualize one of the dominant slogans of the movement; be compelled to replicate what I and a couple of other friends have done when seeing the words "Free Gaza" inelegantly spray-painted on utility boxes in our respective cities: ask an art director to create a tastefully designed, easily removed sticker that reads, "From Terrorists" and neatly place it adjacent to the divisive phrase.

In the three decades that preceded October 7, 2023, Israel experienced the shock of more than one hundred suicide and car bombings aimed against its civilians and soldiers. I'd be happy to provide the exact dates and number of casualities to any college professors or open-minded protestors in search of more balanced data for their courses and convictions. Because if you aren't informed in every respect, another two word slogan, "Never Again," might find these two words spray-painted over it:

"Happened Again."

"Seriously, another Holocaust memoir?"

Although I lose sleep over the very real possibility of Holocaust fatigue, clearly, we will never cease in our efforts to keep its lessons and warnings alive for future generations. We can't let up; the distribution of history is too vital for our own survival and the survival of other oppressed groups in America and around the world. If people tire of reading, we will repackage it as oral histories. And if people grow tired of spoken words, they can now hear the words spoken through holograms of survivors that are programmed using AI and infused with an eerie digital spirit. And, as any anti-Semite will tell you, Jews control the media, so look out streaming services! We have plenty of content ready for optioning.

This thing that I'm writing, just a short book, is one story out of millions told from a Jewish, second-generation perspective. But there's another thing that concerns me as I grind away on this book, which I admit is yet another Holocaust story. I'm talking about the unbelievable horror that began in 1619. Four centuries and still going strong. Black artists have barely scratched the surface on this one. It has never gone away; the racist narrative is so tightly woven into the American backstory, and yet the whole truth still isn't taught in many schools or in textbooks coming out of Texas. Think I'm stretching the truth? In 2015, a Texas textbook taught that blacks were immigrants and workers rather than enslaved people. *Wait. Huh?* That would mean they received wages, and if they received wages, well, they better have paid their taxes dammit. Who do those "workers" think they are, billionaires? But that offense was nearly a decade ago. Surely educators everywhere have moved forward?

Aw, c'mon Florida. Really . . . ? Did you actually say out loud that some Black people benefitted from slavery by picking up useful skills? Oh, I get it, the Plantation system was kind of like DeVry Institute of Technology.

This is a warning to all future Holocaust memoirists: despite the banning of Critical Race Theory curricula, stories of the African American tragedy are finally emerging in a more comprehensive way, expressed across all mediums, and honestly, I'm cheering it on . . . quietly (I don't want a scolding from the Jewish Experience Firsters). Let's face it, the deep pool of creative talent is just getting warmed up.

Anyone seen *12 Years A Slave*? (Thirty-two awards, including three Oscars.) *Beloved*? *Birth of a Nation*? *Django Unchained*? (Okay, Tarantino is white, but that was great.) *Free State of Jones*? *Amistad* (Spielberg, I know . . .) *Get Out*? *Harriet*? And speaking of *Harriet*, Leslie Odom Jr., who played William Still in the movie said this: "You haven't seen the last of *Harriet*. The floodgates have opened; expect more *Harriet* stories, more William Still stories—stories of bravery and cunning to make it to freedom—there are lots of movies in there."

Which means there are lots of reasons why Jewish genocide might find itself relinquishing some of its bookshelf and theater space, passing the torch to other stories that really must be told.

In a way, it's like the Inuit custom of placing the elderly onto floating ice so as not to drain the community's resources. Has that time arrived for the Jewish experience? Will our Holocaust just drift on currents, recede, be forgotten? Will this book be too late? Hang in there, Dad. Ninety is the new eightyish. And I still believe there might be room for a few more tales from our Holocaust.

Treblinka, Forest on the Other Side of Barbed Wire

AS I MENTIONED EARLIER, A SMALL ORCHESTRA PERFORMED DELIGHTFUL music to welcome and relax Jews upon their arrival at the camp. Well, you know what else needs a soundtrack? Their escape.

Two songs come to mind. I will hit the repeat button, turn up the volume, and listen over and over until I complete the in-your-face-and-through-the-fence story of the Treblinka Revolt. Here are two songs and sample lyrics:

> "Uprising" by Muse
> They will not force us
> They will stop degrading us
> They will not control us
> We will be victorious . . .

Also:

> "Start the Riot" by Atari Teenage Riot
> Go!
> Are you ready?
> Start the riot!

Start the riot!
Start the riot!
Start the riot now!
Fight!
War! Fire! Death!
Fuck you! . . .

No muss, no fuss is how the Nazis preferred their extermination process. However, according to eyewitness accounts, not everyone who disembarked from the trains went obediently.

For example, a transport of prisoners arrived at the death camp, but as soon as they stepped off the train cars, they sensed the awful truth. They could smell it; oh, those pesky burning humans—no matter how much you try, you just can't get rid of that embarrassing odor.

The new arrivals mobilized instantly. Fierce fighting broke out. A current of rebellion surged through the impromptu army. They rioted, wild and determined, smashing everything in sight. They broke open chests filled with seized Jewish property. They grabbed sticks, rocks, weapons, and any objects that could be weaponized. There was no time to make a golem. Right away, these Jews vowed to never breathe in the highly concentrated, triple-bonded combo of carbon and oxygen. Better to die in battle.

The offensive went on for hours, but eventually, bullets punctured their valor. By morning, the main yard was littered with the dead and their improvised weapons. Body parts were everywhere. It wasn't enough for the rebels to die of gunshot wounds—many were grotesquely mutilated: limbs torn from their bodies, decapitations, organs spilling out of sword-carved openings. An ugly, inevitable outcome, but still, it was mission accomplished. The rebels circumvented a trip into the gas chambers and, instead, went bravely to the fire.

That was just a warm-up. The official Treblinka Revolt happened on August 2, 1943. The revolt's motto: "Freedom or Death." With their bodies in such weakened conditions, the only chance for freedom (and not death) was to recruit as many bodies as possible to join the revolt and swarm the camp guards like honeybees, which die after stinging.

Survival was unlikely. The odds were about one in six million. A snowball's chance in August in that manufactured hell. But they'd had enough. Time to overwhelm the honey thieves, even if it meant that most of the insurgents would leave their stingers inside their captors' bodies. Everyone understood the losses would be insane, but they were up to their shaved heads in insane. If you do nothing, you die. Revolt, and you'll *probably* die. There was no stopping these seven hundred determined prisoners on the verge of self-liberation.

With the help of a Jewish locksmith, the organizers duplicated a key to the camp's weapon storage facility. The leaders instructed the others to wait for the sound of a grenade; it would serve as an explosive battle cry.

If you could view aerial photos of Treblinka at the time of the revolt, you'd see several serious obstacles. Armed guards were positioned everywhere, on the ground and high above it, carefully observing activities from their watchtower perches. Fences and trenches added an extra layer of fortification against escape. I'd suggest zooming into the aerial photos, but I think we've seen enough piles of smoldering corpses.

Getting back to the logistics . . . I assume you're familiar with the perceived wisdom about people being distracted by shiny objects? Well, turns out it really is true, especially when it came to certain Nazi camp guards. For the revolt to succeed, it was critical to preoccupy the guards who were stationed in watchtowers, because obviously, as soon as the breakout began, bullets would swiftly rain down from their nests.

Here's how a survivor of the revolt described it, and yes, you will slap your palm against your forehead:

"We knew that gold held an immense attraction for them, and they had been doing business with the Jews all the time. So, when the shot rang out, one of the Jews sneaked up to the tower and showed the guard a gold coin. The guard completely forgot that he was on duty. He dropped his machine gun and hastily clambered down to pry the piece of gold from the Jew. The rebels grabbed him, finished him off, and took his revolver. The guards in the other towers were also dispatched quickly."

So, glittering gold worked in their favor. Timing and weather helped as well. It was brutally hot on the day of the escape. To cool off, the Nazi and Ukrainian soldiers left the camp to go swimming at a nearby river. (I'm trying hard not to picture Nazi soldiers in swim trunks from the 1940s—the high elastic waist, straight cut, hugging the upper thigh, basically what your grandma's panties look like.) Anyway, while they were splashing around playing Master Race Marco Polo and having chicken fights, two teenage prisoners took the forged key to the weapons warehouse, broke in, and began passing grenades and firearms through a window.

The prisoners placed the weapons into garbage carts for distribution around the camp. In minutes, Treblinka looked like Alabama or Kentucky or any of those other open carry states in America.

The distribution of arms was going swimmingly as the Nazis splashed about in the river. And then, at 3:35 p.m., the explosion of a grenade—the boom that would begin the battle.

START THE RIOT!

The prisoners set a fuel tank on fire. Barracks and warehouses were torched. Military vehicles were overturned and set ablaze. Grenades were tossed into SS headquarters. For the first time since they'd cut the ribbon at Treblinka, it was Nazi and Ukrainian bodies pressed against the necrotized earth. How tempting to pause for a moment in mid-escape, whip out your circumcised dick, and piss in the face of the dead guards, but there was no time.

Reinforcements were sent in immediately after seeing the fires and hearing the shooting.

Machine-gun fire pierced the air, heading straight toward the fleeing prisoners. The objective was to reach the woods. It was a few miles away. To get there, they'd have to slog across swamps and wild meadows, bullets not far behind, determined to take them down. If they could just reach the woods, they'd have a chance, because that's where the Germans would cease their pursuit. They just halted.

Was it a fear of ticks?

Before the woods, there was wire. So, here's a helpful tip to avoid puncture wounds when escaping from an extermination camp: cover the barbed wire with fabric and clothing before climbing out. It really works! Was the revolt a success? Yes, no, and yes. Yes, because a couple hundred made it over the fence. No, because more than half were killed or captured. Yes, because, of the roughly one hundred Jewish prisoners who managed to escape from Treblinka on that sweltering day in August, nearly seventy survived to see the end of the war. And write about the nightmare. And draw pictures of the nightmare. And speak at schools about the nightmare. And testify at the trials of the men who created the nightmare. And finally, just be able to sleep and not wake up screaming.

Revolt alumni included artists, escape artists, and several former prisoners who went on to publish Treblinka memoirs: Richard Glazer, Jankiel Wiernek, Samuel Willenberg, Chil Rajchman, and Kalman Taigman.

The authors are no longer alive.

> 1972: JANKIEL WIERNEK died in Israel at the age of eighty-three. (Built detailed model of Treblinka death camp currently displayed at the Ghetto Fighter's Museum in Israel.)
>
> 1997: RICHARD GLAZER died in Prague at the age of seventy-seven. (Attended several trials of former SS men, as well as the trial of Franz Stangl, Treblinka's commandant. According to his own testimony, Stangl perceived prisoners not as humans but as cargo that had to be destroyed. He

admitted to mass killings but stated that his "conscience was clear. He was simply doing his duty." Yep, that ol' Topf & Sons cremation oven roasted chestnut.)

*Special shout out to Simon Wiesenthal for that Nazi's capture.

2004: CHIL RAJCHMAN died in Uruguay at the age of eighty-nine. (Worked closely with Office of Special Investigations on the matter of Treblinka guards.)

2012: KALMAN TAIGMAN died in Israel at the age of eighty-eight. (Testified in Eichmann trial.)

2016: SAMUEL WILLENBERG died in Israel at the age of ninety-three. (Went back to Poland, participated in the Warsaw Uprising. Was the guy an uprising adrenaline junkie?)

Thankfully, their stories were shared with the world. There's also, Claude Lanzmann's *Shoah*, the nine-hour documentary that featured rare interviews with Treblinka survivors. That's a whole lot of Holocaust, and mind you, that's just the documentation of life and death in mainly one camp: Treblinka.

Anyone living in the time of Spielberg knows there is a boundless bonanza of Holocaust stories for current and future generations to cram into their brains. They sit on bookshelves and in archives, roll on film and stream on television, not to mention the oral (and now, holographic) histories. Which is why I keep asking myself, is there really room for another story in the collective Holocaust anthology? Perhaps we can squeeze in just one more about this one guy, my father, one of the very last survivors.

No one knows for certain exactly how many Holocaust survivors are still alive today. I can tell you this: whatever that number is, it's on a steep decline.

~~52° 37′51.85″ N, 22° 3′11.01″ E~~
00.0000° N, 00.0000° E
Treblinka, Poland

MID-1940s

THE SOVIETS ENTERED TREBLINKA DURING THE LAST WEEK OF JULY 1944.

Metaphysically speaking, if you liberate a death camp and there's no one there to liberate, can it be called a liberation? Technically speaking, no. Treblinka was not officially liberated. The Nazis did, however, attempt to exterminate the infrastructure of extermination. Before making a break for it, the camp authorities and guards shot the remaining Jewish prisoners (between 300 and 700 people were taken out during the Nazi's last-minute murders and exit strategy). After that, it was full speed ahead with the dismantling and decamping of the camp.

Is it even possible to "disappear" a gruesome enterprise like Treblinka? Not a chance. A death camp is not an ephemeral traveling circus; it can never decompose completely. True, you can wipe away most of the physical parts, but the ghosts and DNA will remain. Nevertheless, the Nazis gave it the old college try.

The first evidence to be erased was the camp's extermination area. However, based on the things they left behind, it's clear that their third-rate cleanup crew sure could have used the services of a Mr. Wolf–type fixer (Harvey Keitel's character in *Pulp Fiction*). Actually, it required someone with far superior skills than even he possessed because this was no fiction; it was one of the most gruesome non-fictions in the history of the world.

Yeah, these morally-depraved incompetents did a half-assed job of leveling the place. They ploughed it over, even planted wild lupins for camouflage, but when Soviet war correspondents investigated the camp, they continually stumbled over pieces of bone protruding from the soil. And, while they did a pretty good job of nimbly avoiding those bones, they also trudged upon human teeth, camp uniform fabrics, building fragments, small mounds of pummeled shoes, mangled human hair, and the anguish still seeping deeply into the earth.

My father, brother, and I entered Treblinka nearly sixty years after the Soviets.

To a certain extent, I was relieved that the murder factories had been pulverized into a coarse dust, forced to conjoin with ashes and souls, forming a viscous alloy of human misery. It would be easier on my father. Best that his eyes did not see the exteriors and fixate on what had occurred inside. There are no foundations or architectural husks to wander through and wonder where, exactly, his father was standing when gas filled the chamber.

But what he did see, well, it broke The Iron Father. Once we got past the symbolic train tracks, closer to the actual site, down to his knees he went. My brother and I immediately reached for him, but he angrily brushed us aside. From that position, he bent over further, and pressed his lips to the wretched parcel of unearthly earth.

"Psst, it kind of looks like Dad is striking a Muslim prayer pose," Steve whispered in my ear.

"Steve, if you fucking dare say that to Dad right now, I guarantee you'll be left behind with these unfortunate souls, maybe under the ground," I warned him. Miraculously, my brother yielded to the better angels of his nature in this satellite office of Hell.

At any rate, what Treblinka lacks in physical evidence, it makes up in haunted. An unshakable sense of eerie torment is especially palpable as you approach the twenty-six-foot-high stone memorial, an ascending centerpiece on the table of the damned. This prominent part of the Treblinka camp was not designed to provide solace or make space for quiet contemplation. The revenants will never allow it. They insist that you hear their spectral cries. It is a loud, melancholic hum that intermingles with your agitated breathing, impossible to turn off.

We covered our ears, but the steady drone of suffering, that woeful dissonant buzz of unfinished prayers, bores right through your fingers. When you stand before the monument, you are standing on the spot where the gas chambers once stood.

Behind the main monument is a different monument. It is lower in height; in fact, it presses firmly to the earth.

Measuring 22 meters long and 4.5 meters wide, the rectangular mixed-media installation has a blackened tar-like surface: a deathly icing constructed of crushed black basalt meant to symbolize burnt charcoal and charred human remains. Which makes perfect sense since actual human ashes are one of the materials mixed into this flat grave marker designed to place you at the edge of a cremation pit.

Those are two of the monuments that we confronted when we came to the Treblinka death camp.

There are others. 17,000 to be more precise. Most of this blood-sweat-tear-carbon monoxide-stained parcel of secluded Polish land is a vast symbolic cemetery comprised of 17,000 jagged stones that are affectingly designed to resemble gnarled headstones. There are two explanations for the huge number. The first is that the 17,000 stones represent the highest number of Jews gassed in a single day. The other states that 17,000 represents the number of Jewish communities destroyed in the Holocaust. Seven hundred of the stones are inscribed with the names of villages and communities that were forced to send their people to the camps. As we weaved our way among the markers of mass death, we couldn't help but notice the sea of smaller stones without city or town names etched into them. They represent the villages in Poland where all Jewish life was extinguished. Steve and I remained stone cold silent. My father, on the other hand, was in a muttering loop: "Oh my God." "I'm so sorry." "Papa, Papa." "Oh my God." "I'm so sorry." "Papa, Papa."

At some point during our self-guided tour (we were the only visitors at the site), my father suggested we split up—he wanted to be alone; it was a lot for him to manage. My brother ventured to the edges of the camp. I wandered off as well but made certain my father was visible to me, just in case. Just in case what, you're wondering? A lot of things flew into my mind—a broken heart, a hypertensive crisis, a bulge in the brain. *But he's a . . . survivor. He'll survive this,* I told myself. So I continued my wandering among the dead and finally found a stone-free place to sit. But I couldn't remain seated. I couldn't stand either.

Something pulled me closer to the ground. Think horror movie, last scene, hand reaches up from a grave and grabs me by the T-shirt, yanks me down. No bullshit. This really happened, and it pissed me off because I'm very particular about my black T-shirts. I don't care if you are a Holocaust haunter, do not stretch out the collar, wraith.

I lay on my back. Blue sky and biting flies hovered above me. Really? Is this really about to happen? Am I about to throw pebbles at God's window, hoping They/Them will open it and provide some sort of spiritual guidance? Will this be the moment when I reconnect to my faith? I rolled my head to the left, then rolled it to the right. Silence. No sign.

Okay, then, I will sing "Avenu Malkenu," the Barbra Streisand version; if Barbra can't summon God, then who can? I did sing, in a whisper, but still no response. All righteee, Lord, I guess you're making me push the big red button, go bar mitzvah *haftorah* on your perfect omnipotence. Oh God, no, no, no . . . What if I mangle it the way my brother did? Will God and the ectoplasmic entourage go after Steve, or worse, come for my father?

Okay, ready, here we go, just gotta relax, maybe tee things up with some pre-*haftorah* blessings:

"Barechu et Adonai ham'vorach . . . "

(*Praised be Adonai, who is blessed for ever and ever.*)

Suddenly, a chorus of voices rise from the dead.

It's . . . it's the ghosts of Treblinka choir. What on ash-soaked earth is happening?

They respond with: "Baruch Adonai ham'vorach l'olam vaed."

Ohhhhhhkay . . . um: "Baruch atah, Adonai Eloheinu, Melech hao-lam, asher bachar bin'vi-im tovim, v'ratzah v'divreihem hane-emarim be-emet. Baruch atah, Adonai, habocher baTorah uv'Moshe avdo, uv'Yisrael amo, uvin'vi- ei ha-emet vatzedek." *(Praise to You, Adonai our God, Sovereign of the universe, who has chosen faithful prophets to speak words of truth. Praise to You, Adonai, for the revelation of Torah, for Your servant Moses, for Your people Israel and for prophets of truth and righteousness.)*

Are you feeling it, Creator? Need some more? So you want me to demonstrate that I have not abandoned the faith, huh? I cleared my throat to make room for all the chhh chhh *chaftorah* sounds about to soar into Treblinka's eerie atmosphere.

Ready, here we go:

"Rani v'simchi bat tziyon . . . " And on and on.

(Sing and be glad "daughter" of Zion, Jerusalem, "we" the exiled nation of Israel, is returning home . . .)

"AHHHMEN!" crooned the choir.

Nailed it! Well, whaddaya know? I remembered every single Hebrew word and inflection. And it worked; the phantoms of Treblinka broke their hold and finally let go of my collar. Phew, they didn't stretch it out.

I rolled up the air Torah scroll and waited for the judgment, fully expecting God to assess my *haftorah* performance the way Simon Cowell would—encouraging, but at the same time pointing out areas that needed improvement. Silence. I tried to have a transcendental conversation. I invited an almighty critique. But it was clear there was no God in this God-forsaken place. Just me and my brother. My father. And the phantasmal voices of the departed.

Oh shit, my father! Where's my father? Of course. He had found the largest symbolic stone in the symbolic cemetery. Etched into the rock was the word "Warsaw." He was touching it, then kissing the part of his hand that made contact with the stone. He was leaning against the rock, pressing into it. From my flattened vantage point, I could see his head was bowed, his shoulders shaking. He is singing the *Kaddish*, the Jewish prayer for the dead.

With eyes on our father, Steve and I asked ourselves over and over, *Why are we here*? Why did we come to this dreadful place, back to this crime scene? What were we thinking bringing him here? We knew it would hurt him. Deeply. What the hell were we thinking? We struggled with the question. It was a huge question, the kind of question that vexes small, somewhat traumatized minds like ours.

It took a few minutes, but then it came to me. I realized why we were here; we were here so that our father and his father could finally say goodbye.

Chinese Restaurant

FOSTER CITY, CALIFORNIA

The check is placed on the table. My father fake reaches for his wallet, fake attempting to pay.

DAD

Thanks, boys, that was a good meal. Happy birthday to me. You got enough to finally finish your father's epic tale of chasing tail, taking beatings, outfoxing Nazis, and living to tell about it?

I close the notebook, tap it twice.

TODD

Think I do, Pops; it's basically a pornographic true crime story with a few scenes of genocide and statehood building. Thanks for filling in most of the blanks about your experiences.

My father's eyes widen. He has a thought to share.

DAD

You wanna know what'll shoot you straight to the top of Amazon's Holocaust category, Todd? Change the title to *Dave's Tomatoes*.

Steve is polishing off the last half of his fortune cookie as he responds.

STEVE

Silly me, I was hoping Genetically Inherited Holocaust Trauma might skip a generation.

TODD

Sorry Steve, Dad seems just fine, but man, did those terrorized genes do a number on us. Hey Dad?

DAD

Oh boy . . . What, Todd?

TODD

Just one last question. It's about that Israeli soldier. The sexy, homicidal hottie—

DAD

No more. The Answer Store is closed. But nice try.

Stuffed with food that was righteously declared free of MSG, we walk out of the restaurant and hug goodbye. But first, we had to button our pants.

Group Text

ME, REID, LAUREN

PAPA: You guys got a few minutes, it's REALLY, REALLY IMPORTANT.

REID (nineteen hours later): Yeah, what's up, you good?

LAUREN (twenty-five hours later): Hi, everything ok?

PAPA: One thing I clearly passed onto you guys . . . traumatically chronic lateness.

REID: Haha

LAUREN: Ha, sorry

PAPA: It's about your grandfather.

REID: Oh no, is he sick?

LAUREN: ?????!!!!!

PAPA: He's fine. Talked to him this morning. But I made the mistake of bringing up Jerusalem Day and Israel and the ongoing conflict.

LAUREN: That set him off?

PAPA: Oh yeah. During his tirade, I received three "putzfaces," two "schmucks," but only one "schmendrick."

REID: Disappointing, try harder.

PAPA: I will. My goal is to set the record for number of "putzfaces" in a single conversation.

REID: You can do it, Papa, I believe in you.

PAPA: So, I need you guys to be totally honest about something. It's a Holocaust thing.

LAUREN: OMG Reid, imagine that . . . Papa bringing up the Holocaust.

REID: He probably gets notifications on his watch . . . "Time to Stand and Talk About Nazis."

PAPA: Exactly. And so glad you guys are saying that. Because here's what I need to know . . . Okay, so, unlike me, you guys were told about your grandfather's story at a very early age. How do you think that affected you?

REID: Hmm, well, I was potty training at the time. You scared the crap right out of me, which probably sped things up. So thanks, I guess?

PAPA: Nice. And if I used emojis . . . eyeroll face.

LAUREN: Well, while most of my friends were falling asleep to the goofy rhymes of Dr. Seuss, I was drifting off to passages from When Hitler Stole Pink Rabbit . . .

PAPA: Part of my master plan . . . introduce the Holocaust pathogen early into your developing minds, inoculate you against the tough realities of life. And it worked.

LAUREN: Meh.

DOCTOR'S NOTE

Dear Reid and Lauren, Please excuse your father's unorthodox parenting skills. One of the major themes that characterizes the parent-child relationship of Holocaust Survivor Offspring is survival issues (e.g. overprotection and fear of separation).

—Best regards,
Dr. Scharf and Dr. Mayseless

Chinese Restaurant

FOSTER CITY, CALIFORNIA

I SIT OPPOSITE STEVE. THE SEAT USUALLY OCCUPIED BY MY FATHER IS vacant. This time I want to speak with my brother without being called a putz or a shmendrick. Not that I usually mind. In fact, I sometimes sign my name Todd P. (or S.) Diamond—an inside joke that puts a smile on my face each time I do it, although the hotel clerk or waiter may view my standalone giddiness as the mark of someone who's a little off. At any rate, I have a few questions for which I may already know the answer, but it's reassuring to hear it played back by someone else, someone on the inside. So:

TODD

Do you think we'd have survived his traumas? Would we have had the balls to take the chances he did?

Steve tilts his head, then pushes his tongue through his middle and index fingers.

TODD

What's that look? Yeah, well, maybe I'm a pussy. But I wonder how you or I might've been different under the circumstances he faced. I mean, we can never really know in advance, can we? And if we survived without going off the rails, would anyone seeing us here today ever think we—or Dad—were anything but just folks who're out for dinner and had a hunky-dory American dream life? Let's face it, we're holograms to strangers; they don't see our history, and they can't understand what's going on inside. To the uninitiated, it appears to be all pretty normal. Drumroll. Pause.

Except that it wasn't.

STEVE

Maybe it was the farmer's daughter who set the tone. He was what, thirteen? I didn't get into the saddle until I was seventeen, and then, well, let's say I fell off it pretty quickly.

TODD

Dad always said that if you're a real man, you "die in the saddle."

STEVE

Who does he think we are, the Rockefellers? I bet Nelson's secretary felt awful about causing the tycoon's heart-stopping, traumatic orgasm.

TODD

Yeah, okay, but seriously . . . the Ghetto, pretending to be a gentile, getting away with it, being almost adopted by one of the few families who didn't think he personally killed Christ, just, well, surviving, making his way to Israel only to be caught up in another war, then coming here, starting over, a new language, culture, politics. And in the end, living, for all intents and purposes, a regular life. I don't know. I'm not so sure I could've survived if that shoe were on one of my feet.

STEVE

It's not about surviving; it's about living. And you never know how you'd act or react. You can't project. Pass the pork dumplings.

TODD

On *shabbat*, no less.

STEVE

God said on the sixth day, 'you gotta eat, put some meat on your bones, not that you should be *zaftig*, mind you.'

TODD

Glory be to the Lipitor. Sure, Steve, we got his features all right, but did we get his balls?

STEVE

Can't say I've ever looked. And hey, just be thankful we were never in a situation where it was necessary to reverse the handiwork of a *mohel*.

Todd looks down at the napkin on his lap. Pats the family jewels–the cut Diamond.

TODD

Seriously, what do we inherit?

STEVE

You mean other than a ten-year-old Pontiac with less than 25,000 miles on it?

TODD

Do they make Pontiacs anymore?

STEVE

I always liked them because the mascot on the hood looked like Uncle Ike.

TODD

Minus the scar.

STEVE

Hey, I'll arm wrestle you for Dad's Lladro Moses figurine.

TODD

You think it's a sign that a big chunk of the Ten Commandments tablet broke off?

STEVE

I can't remember which one. Was it 'Honor your father and mother?'

TODD

Probably 'Thou shalt not kill.'
So what is it . . . gumption? Determination?

STEVE

Maybe it was naiveté or possibly bullheadedness. Not saying those are negative things, by the way.

TODD

So we're one half of his genes. Maybe that gets us 50 percent of his perseverance. You know what that means? Our kids get only a quarter. Each generation dilutes the one that comes after. Maybe that's a good thing. At least in terms of trauma, anyway. I'd like to think that the *mishigas* that Dad went through doesn't have to be automatically passed down. We get to create our own and inflict that special damage on our kids. And so on, down the line.

STEVE

I know it took years to get "most" of his story, but Dad did us a favor by letting us in on what he went through.

TODD

I'm thinking it was a teaching lesson. One that I had to learn so that I can pass the test.

STEVE

The test of what?

TODD

Life.

Steve drains his scotch (on the rocks). Todd knocks back his scotch (neat). Neither brother makes a move to pick up the check.

A final thought:

As a parent and the son of a survivor, I'm relieved to know that nearly all my family's Holocaust trauma resides in bitter ol' Jew me. Evidently, my prescription for third-generation Holocaust homeopathy worked like the blood of a lamb, because the trauma wasn't passed on—it mostly passed over.

DOCTOR'S NOTE:

To the Children of Todd Diamond,

Please excuse your father's conduct, manner, and at times, nonconforming methods of parenting. Studies have reported that Holocaust offspring may experience a range of behavioral difficulties. These include low self-esteem, catastrophizing, anxiety, nightmares, dysphoria, guilt, hypervigilance, interpersonal difficulties, depression, aggression, anger, and self-destructive behavior.

But it's not just trauma that affects genetic expression in subsequent generations. If told thoughtfully and with deep affection, one's family story can foster an enduring resiliency.

It has the power to change everything.

—Sincerely,
your dad and the researchers at Mount Sinai

Appendix of the Righteous

The Farmer Who Saved Ike and Bella

When someone you adore passes away, the distress can ship you forgotten memories faster than Amazon Prime same-day delivery. Bella died two years ago; she was ninety-nine years old. Immediately after my father received the news, I received the sound of the ringtone I set for his calls (*Old Car Horn*), in my AirPods. I was in a café at the time, working on an ad campaign for a stock investment start-up. They were promoting their Custodial Accounts: Owned by a minor but managed by a parent. I couldn't imagine what it would be like if my father was supervising my childhood stock picks. Actually, I did imagine, and it goes something like this:

"McDonald's, who'd eat that crap? Ach, such a putz. That company will be out of business within a year."

"Xerox? The only time you used one of those machines was to take a picture of your ass. You want a good investment . . . gold."

The moment I heard my father's voice, I knew someone had died.

"Bella, my beautiful *tante* Bella. Her daughter just let me know. That's it, Todd, there's not much left of our family," my father said sadly.

Bella was always so kind to my father. She took him in right after the war. Bella also cooked the most delicious brisket, which she delivered to his Brooklyn apartment at least once a month as my father was starting out in America.

I remember the Sunday visits to Ike and Bella's house in New Jersey. I'd hang out in the basement with Ike watching football. He was a man of very, very few words. The way he best expressed himself was at the stereo turntable. The man had an impressive vinyl collection, most of it classical, most of it super melancholy shit. He'd drop the needle, walk over to his reclining chair, close his eyes, and get lost in the music. That's when I'd head upstairs; the guy kind of creeped me out. Now, of course, I have a better idea of the images dancing in his mind to those soundtracks.

"After Ike died, did Bella talk much about their experiences in hiding?" I asked him.

"Rarely. It's too hard. You have to bury that stuff and carry on," he responded.

There was a long pause, then he was suddenly jolted by a memory about Ike. Surprise, it's actually a nice one. Bet you didn't expect that.

"Sure, Ike was a prick, a callous son-of-a-bitch, but every now and then, he shined," my father said.

"Hmm, seems to me his moral compass aligned with the North Pole of Uranus," I replied.

Youranus . . . Immediately I thought about all the photocopies of my ass made on Xerox machines throughout the years; you could fill an entire museum wing with those pieces of (f)art.

Then the shocker: My father told me how, in the late sixties, Ike reached out to the farmer who took on the immense risk of hiding the war-fused lovers to finally thank him for the fine accommodations in the underground Survival Suite. So Ike brought the farmer's entire family to New York for three weeks.

Ike was successful; he had the big house. He owned several hardware stores; money wasn't an issue. Ike paid for everything—the hotel, the restaurants. He took the farmer's family to all the big tourist spots: the Empire State Building, Times Square, Radio City Music Hall, Katz's Delicatessen, the Statue of Liberty.

And get this . . . before the farmer and his family boarded the plane back to Poland, Ike handed him a box; it was filled with gold coins and many hundred-dollar bills.

Sure, Ike might have lacked emotional currency, but in the end, he expressed his gratitude by giving the farmer something that he truly valued.

The Warsaw Police Captain

Last year, my father had the opportunity to share his story with representatives from the Israeli Consulate in San Francisco. They heard a brief summary about his early life through the head of Jewish Family and Children's Services, a group that my father belongs to.

The Israeli representatives wanted to hear more, so they hopped into their fortified Mercedes and drove over to San Mateo, to my father's apartment. The representatives were deeply moved by the bravery of the police officer that helped my father in Germany and said they'd use all of their influence and connections to track down the righteous captain's family, to honor him for helping our family and our people.

Furthermore, the Israeli Consulate promised my father they would provide him with an all-expenses-paid trip to Israel. Um, still waiting on that promise to be filled, guys.

Steve, My Brother.

The earliest memory I can retrieve from my life's hard drive is a story about my brother. I was three years old. I'm unable to recall a memory from a younger age. Really, though, why would anyone want to venture further back than that?

Although, if it were possible, I'd want to remember the sensation of being bathed in a kitchen sink, a damp washcloth gently exfoliating the crud and cigarette ash from my scalp. I only know this because Baby

Todd's photo album had two pictures of me in this situation; in both images, my mother's beehive hairdo was partially out of frame, but the dangling cigarette with its glowing red-hot tip and plank of gray ash *was* in the picture, and it was awfully close to baby's head.

Back to year three.

This is where it starts, the very first thing I can remember. It's a memory about furniture: a towering bedroom dresser. My tiny three-year-old hands grab the scuffed brass handles of the bottom drawer. I struggle and shake the thing, determined to get it open. It opens just enough for me to catch the scent of cedar chips and musty wool sweaters. The cheaply made pine colossus was not standing for it.

Down it came at me, ready to pulverize a curious tot. And, like a panicked villager being chased by a disastrous tsunami running toward the photojournalist's camera, I hauled my recently potty-trained ass out of there, never looking back.

I should've heard a muffled crash, a sound softened by plush carpet. But all I heard were grunts and tortured breathing followed by a call for help to my mother who was in the kitchen preparing a dinner of spaghetti with ketchup sauce, delicately seasoned with Pall Mall cigarette ash.

My brother had swooped in, an asthmatic superhero. He caught the toppling chest in mid-fall. No cape, no tights, just a short-of-breath-eight-year-old with thin, straining arms.

Steve, my older brother, my first glimpse of the righteous.

"My Grandfather's Story"

BY LAUREN DIAMOND

I'M NOT THE FIRST PERSON TO WRITE ABOUT MY FATHER'S REMARKABLE life. My daughter, Lauren, a third-generation survivor and granddaughter of Poppy Dave, beat me to it by eleven years. She was barely a teenager when she kicked off his story like this:

> *David sat down at the table across from me and took a large sip of the beverage beside him. As I asked the first question, he looked away, the deep, soft lines I usually see in his face hardened. All too clearly, I could see the hesitant sadness in his eyes as he braced himself to revisit his past. David took a deep breath and then slowly, a small, unexpected smile spread across his face as he folded his hands and turned to me.*
>
> *My grandfather, David Diamond, had a formidable childhood growing up in the midst of World War II, and then experienced a different perspective of life, fighting with the IDF in the Israeli War of Independence.*
>
> *Eventually he moved to America to create a new life for himself but faced new obstacles he would have to overcome. Despite many difficult situations that have arisen throughout David's life, he has managed to pick himself up, stay a positive person, and most importantly, survive.*

Many of the gruesome details do not appear in the biography she wrote about her grandfather. They were intentionally softened in their transfer from first to third generation. The naughty bits were withheld as well. Thanks, Dad. You have no idea how much I appreciate your discretion.

My father with his father.
Before being moved to the Warsaw Ghetto.

My father in Warsaw before the war.

My father, a.k.a. Tadeusz Lipski, fake identity papers.

David during Israel's War of Independence.

David (upper right) with friends from Kibbutz Ramat Yohanan, including Shlomo (bottom right).

In 2023, my father received a special award from the Friends of the IDF. When I asked him what he did to earn such an honor, he simply said, "Really, putzface?"

Acknowledgments

For more than two years, my father was a slave laborer. Brutal work for no money. His dreadful experiences are the inspiration behind these acknowledgments. You see, for some reason, several of the smartest people I know took time out of their busy lives to read this thing and offer insights. For free. Seriously, none of them have sent an invoice. This includes my brother, Steve Diamond (he's family; he had no choice).

The three Scotts: Silverstein, Triedman, and Haltzman. Although they sound like a Jewish law firm when lumped together, each offered a great perspective. Actually, Scott Triedman and Scott Haltzman (author of four books on marriage and family relationships) are admired medical professionals. Scott Silverstein is a lawyer and entrepreneur who is married to Amy Silverstein. Yes, *that* Amy Silverstein, who has written two bestselling books including the powerful *My Glory Was I Had Such Friends*. What a gift having her read the manuscript. Amy's comments were a masterclass in writing, which I sorely needed. She will be sorely missed.

Thank you, Leo Bottary, for the fastest read and feedback on the book, plus insights on the publishing world. Leo just published his third thought-provoking business book. Brian Murphy, thank you for reading and enlightening me on the very real condition of Genetically Inherited Trauma. Alyn Carlson, an artist and actor whose unique lens perceived this as both a book and a play. She sees art and the world in multihued multidimensions.